DEVELOPING METHODS OF INQUIRY:

A Source Book for Elementary Media Personnel

by

Nancy Polette

The Scarecrow Press, Inc.

Metuchen, N. J.   1973

Library of Congress Cataloging in Publication Data

Polette, Nancy.
    Developing methods of inquiry.

    Includes bibliographies.
    1. Instructional materials centers. I.   Title.
LB3044.P64   027.82'22   72-11992
ISBN 0-8108-0575-8

CONTENTS

FOREWORD

The seventies might well be termed the "Era of Uncertainty" in the educational world. Caught up amid the conflicting philosophies of Perennialism, Progressivism and Reconstructionism, the school librarian or media specialist must be a combination of diplomat extraordinaire and super salesman to initiate and administer an instructional materials program that will prove effective in the educational process.

This book is an attempt to provide practical guidance for media personnel in determining prevailing philosophies in the individual school situation, in establishing a philosophy of media center service based on the development of a strong methods of inquiry program, and in initiating such a program --one that will hopefully prove to be successful through understanding and working through the positive aspects of prevailing school philosophies, whatever they may be.

The reader will find that practical application is stressed rather than educational theory per se and that where possible, educational jargon has been avoided in favor of the introduction of clear models for action. In summary, Developing Methods of Inquiry presents THE CHALLENGE, THE PROCESS, and THE TOOLS in order that the Instructional Materials Center may serve as an important catalyst for change in the schools.

Chapter 1

PHILOSOPHIES WHICH DETERMINE
EDUCATIONAL PROGRAMS

Defining Terms

A speaker at a recent meeting of school librarians
found himself in a quandary as to the best approach for ad-
dressing the group. He debated on the wisdom of beginning
his talk by bringing greetings to his fellow librarians, since,
in the educational vernacular of the day, librarians are no
longer librarians but have assumed such titles as media
specialist, or resource specialist, or instructional materials
center director, or perhaps, materials coordinator. The
enterprising speaker decided that all of these terms were
based on the idea that media people deal with sources of information regardless of form, and he began his talk by bringing greetings to his fellow "sorcerers"!

This may not be such a misnomer, for the current
educational scene is one of such change that the media specialist must indeed be a sorcerer to bring together and unite
the diverse modes of thinking found in any educational complex today.

Hopefully, the educational community is achieving a
level of sophistication where it is understood that the school
library (assuming it is a modern school library) is not simply a storehouse of print materials, but contains a variety of
print and nonbook materials including films, filmstrips, loops,
maps, globes, tapes (reel-to-reel and cassette), records,
microforms, models, picture sets, art prints, study prints,
realia and any other media which will assist students in developing concepts independently. This same level of sophistication should apply to school media personnel. The school
librarian, in order to be effective today, must show expertise in both print and nonprint areas. Certainly, the school
librarian must be a resource person in every sense of the
term.

1

Thus, the terms "library" and "instructional materials center" are used synonymously in this book, as are the terms "librarian" and "media specialist."

The Challenge

School librarians as a group are possibly among the most dedicated, well-trained, zealous, hardworking and long-suffering members of the educational team of the school. The constant refrain of the school librarian (or media specialist) is paradoxical. On the one hand is the often heard statement, "The work load is so great that it is impossible to render the kind of service for which I was trained." This, however, is closely followed by the librarians' lament: "I cannot understand why teachers don't use all of the resources available to them. If the kids were only turned loose, how much more they'd learn!" One might assume from the latter that the typical school librarian's workload consists of keeping unused, dusty shelves free of termites, and oiling idle hardware on the off-chance that a request for it might be received.

The actual situation in most school libraries is only somewhat better than this. The librarian's time is probably spent for the most part in processing and circulating materials--two tasks which are chiefly clerical in nature.

In many schools throughout the nation the librarian is looked upon, by administrators and teachers alike, not as an educator but as an organizer and expediter of materials. Countless administrators can see no reason for purchasing processed materials or even for purchasing printed catalog cards when an "expert" is on hand to do the job. Many teachers show no dismay, and even expect, that the librarian will be spending time behind a charge desk circulating materials. The situation in the elementary school library is even more disastrous. Faculty members who look upon the elementary materials center as a "place where children get books to read for fun," see the elementary librarian as incidental to this process. Indeed, why hire a librarian at all when volunteer mothers are available for the job?

What is needed is an examination of the philosophies that govern the educational process in any particular school. While it is assumed that administrators, faculty members, and school librarians all speak the English language, it is doubtful that they all understand it to the same degree.   Understanding is totally dependent on philosophy.   Take, for example, a statement found in most school district policy books:

> Education must provide the opportunity, incentive, and atmosphere for each pupil to develop mentally, physically, morally and socially to the fullest extent of his abilities.

The Perennialist administrator or teacher would interpret this statement to mean that the abilities the child should develop are those of conforming to a basic set of predetermined principles, of acquiring certain basic truths and of accepting and following basic rules laid down by the authority in charge.

To the Progressive educator the statement says that every child shall reach his full potential for discovery and creativity, and for developing the ability to think critically, as well as acquiring the ability to adapt to an ever-changing environment.

In the view of the Reconstructionist, the child's abilities should be developed to enable him to live in harmony in the world village of the future and to understand the social and cultural forces which shape his life.

It is important, then, for school media personnel to be able to define and recognize the basic modes of thinking prevalent in the school, and to develop a clear philosophy of education as it concerns the role of the media center.   For this purpose, a brief examination of these philosophies follows.

Perennialism

The traditionalist educator approaches the teaching-learning process with highly structured tenets.   He believes in the unchanging quality of human nature and in the resulting constancy of education.   Based on the Realism of Francis Bacon, John Locke and Jean-Jacques Rousseau, the Perennialist philosophy maintains that man's distinguishing characteristic is his reason, and thus, education should concentrate on developing rationality.   Basic skills and factual information are important to the traditionalist for he believes

that truth is unchanging and must be instilled in students
through instruction in basic subjects. Authority is unchal-
lenged, rigid and uncompromising, and students have no control over the learning process. To one who holds this type
of reasoning, the suggestion that the student should be allowed to explore, to discover, and to develop his own reasoning powers through following a process of critical thinking is nothing short of a proposal of anarchy in the schools!

Implications of Perennialism for the School Library

The traditionalist or perennialist teacher views the
school library as a storehouse of the world's knowledge, or
of basic truths which have been handed down in written form
through the ages. The librarian is seen as "the keeper of
the key" to this storehouse, and one who organizes and as-
sures the careful maintenance of order, both within the collection itself and in the realm of human behavior. The
stereotype of the school librarian has evolved from this
traditionalist role. She is the kind, mouselike, little old
lady whose total vocabulary seems to consist of a single
sound made by placing the teeth together, pressing a finger
to the lips, and emitting a shhhh! Traditionalist teachers
and librarians look upon the library as a place where students are welcome to sample the world's knowledge as long
as the sample comes from a highly structured reading list
of some sort, listing materials which are sure to contain
those basic truths that the teacher wishes to impart. The
introduction of nonbook materials into this hallowed realm
of learning is considered "nothing but frills" at best, and at
worst, sacrilegious.

It would seem that the Perennialists have refused to
acknowledge the electronic world in which we live and the
fact that the young, who have cut their teeth on television
and have learned to toddle with the stereo and tape recorder,
are most comfortable in the electronically motivated learning situation. For them the printed word has been a minor
factor in the acquisition of information.

Progressivism

It has often been noted that in Colleges of Education
prospective teachers learn the theories of Progressivism
well. However, the traditionalist practices by which most
of them were taught are so well ingrained that these are the

teaching methods that are actually put into effect when the
learner becomes the teacher. Progressivism, or the application of John Dewey's Pragmatism to education, has had its
peaks and valleys of popularity on the educational scene and
is possibly the most misinterpreted and misunderstood of all
educational philosophies. Dewey defines education in this
manner:

> It is the reconstruction or reorganization of experi-
> ence which adds to the meaning of experience, and
> which increases the ability to direct the course of
> subsequent experience. [1]

The Progressive teacher rejects the authoritarian role
and serves as a counselor or guide. He believes that children learn best when intrinsically motivated, and that education is an active process with this intrinsic motivation stem-
ming from the needs of the individual. The student learns,
not through rote memorization, but through problem-solving
activities. Since education is considered to be life itself,
students must learn cooperation in a democratically-struc-
tured situation. Students are encouraged to express their
ideas and to develop by means of problem-solving activities
a conceptual approach to education.

Implications of Progressivism for School Library Services

The implications of Progressivism for the role of the
library or materials center in the educational process are
many. True problem-solving activities require the use of a
variety of media for investigation and experimentation. Subjects under investigation must be exposed to diverse view-
points and, in selecting relevant ideas from a mass of material, distinguishing the significant from the less significant,
and fact from opinion, as well as assessing the accuracy and
authority of the source used, the student undergoes an in-
tegrative process of critical thinking. Not only does the
Progressive teacher require extensive library facilities, but
his students spend more time using these facilities than is
spent in the classroom.

Where extensive use of a variety of resources is required, it follows that helping students to acquire problem-
solving skills and to develop methods of inquiry is one of
the major roles of the school librarian.

Reconstructionism

The Reconstructionist philosophy, as formulated by
Theodore Brameld, commits itself to the complete change of
society. The Reconstructionist advocates a program of
social reform of a truly democratic nature and stresses the
need for a restructuring of education based on the findings
of the behavioral scientists. The Reconstructionist determines desirable behavioral goals for the student and places
stress on the means of achieving these goals. Emphasis is
on the future. Many educators accept the idea that it is desirable to identify educational outcomes in behavioral terms
and firmly believe that such objectives can be determined in
advance of any teaching-learning situation. The learning
process can then be programmed for successful achievement
of these objectives. Evidence of the Reconstructionist philosophy can be found in several new issues which are hotly debated among educators today; accountability (which measures
educational progress by output rather than by input), the role
of electronically based learning activities, the educational
model, and performance contracting.

Certainly most educators would agree that our educational system is long overdue for an overhaul. The social
changes brought about by the speeding up of communication,
technological development, and urbanization have created a
totally interdependent society. It is no longer possible (if
indeed it ever was) to fill the human mind with the world's
knowledge. Thus the Reconstructionists see the ability to
acquire information rapidly as an essential factor in achieving behavioral objectives.

Implications of Reconstructionism for the School Library

For the rapid acquisition of information a variety of
materials is essential. It is the outcome of the learning
situation, not the process, with which the Reconstructionist
is concerned. Sophisticated information retrieval systems
which speed up the processes of location and acquisition are
considered essential. Computer assisted instruction is seen
as a way of providing quick and efficient acquisition of skills.

An additional service of the materials center is to
make available to the teacher learning packages based on
specific behavioral objectives. The role of the media center
in this type of educational climate is that of supplying instant

information in a variety of forms, and the media center
staff must be able to demonstrate expertise in computer
technology as it relates to specified learning outcomes.

Humanism

Most philosophers would not accept Humanism as a
basic philosophy; however, the past decade has seen the rise
of Humanistic thought among educators. A Humanistic
approach to education is most easily achieved by the Progressive teacher who sees his class, not as a group of
students but as unique individuals with diverse backgrounds,
abilities, interests, motivations and needs. To the Humanist
it is not nearly so important what a child learns as how he
feels about the learning situation. The Humanist returns to
the idea of the necessity for intrinsic rather than extrinsic
motivation, and learning activities based on the needs and
interests of the individual. The building of a positive self-
concept on the part of each child is considered the most
important part of the educative process, and learning activities are structured toward the development of this positive
self-image.

The Implications of Humanism for School Library Services

In fostering a Humanistic approach to education the
school library serves as a warm, inviting place for the individual pursuit of knowledge. It will contain a variety of
media on the many achievement and interest levels found
among students in a particular educational complex, and the
librarian and teacher will work together to see that the child
makes positive achievement toward his goals, using those
materials with which he will be most comfortable and most
successful. The helping hand of the librarian is always
near and the role of the librarian is that of master teacher
and counselor whose knowledge of the learning process, the
curriculum, the materials and the students is utilized in
helping each learner toward the successful achievement of
his objectives.

Taking the School's Philosophical Temperature

In reviewing briefly the educational philosophies prevailing in the schools today it should be easy to see why

many library programs spend a good deal of time warming
up but never get off the ground. Let us return to the example of the traditionalist administrator who cannot see the
value in either purchasing processed materials or expending
funds for sufficient clerical help to do the job when a librarian has (to his way of thinking) been hired for this purpose. Here we have a perfect example of the clash of philosophies which is at the root of the problem. It may seem
to be a case of the irresistible force (the Progressive librarian) meeting the immovable object (the Perennialist administrator). Yet, to the administrator, his position, based
on his philosophy, is perfectly defensible. He does not see
the librarian's role as a master teacher but as one who ac-
quires and organizes materials. He fully expects the librarian's time to be spent in organization. And if students
in the school are using library resources to acquire only
those materials specified by teachers to acquire certain
basic facts, then this is indeed the role of the school librar-
ian--to secure and organize materials so that they are accessible at the required moment.

On the other hand, the Progressive librarian looks
forward to a media center allowing free and open access to
all materials. A constant and unscheduled flow of students
seeking individual assistance in problem-solving activities and
in developing the skills of critical thinking is both expected
and desirable. The librarian's need to be free of routine
clerical tasks, to work directly with students and teachers in
the discovery process and in developing methods of inquiry,
is seen as the primary objective of good library service. A
satisfactory merging of these diverse philosophies can be
achieved only when the existence of the philosophies is recognized. And such philosophies can be recognized if one is
aware of the signs to be observed in a tour of any educational institution.

The Closed School

In the closed school the principal is the supreme
authority and faculty members and students have little part
in any decision-making process. Classrooms are self-contained and materials are few, with the exception of the basic
textbook in each discipline, and this is almost totally relied
upon for the dispensing of information. Teachers' guides
are followed rigorously and plan books are made out one to
two weeks in advance and submitted to the principal for

approval. Student desks follow a uniform pattern of placement (usually in rows) and time slots are set aside for every
activity of the day and are adhered to without change. A
system of bells heralds the end of one activity and the beginning of the next. Individual students are rarely found in
the halls, and class groups enter and leave the building in
straight lines, accompanied by the teacher.

The library or materials center is a model of order
(if it exists at all) and consists almost entirely of books plus
perhaps a few periodicals. If nonbook materials are found
in the center they are exclusively for the use of faculty
members, who are supposedly better guardians of these materials than are the students. Weekly or bi-weekly library
periods are scheduled for each class and are structured so
that the librarian can relay to the students specific information predetermined by what the librarian and/or teacher feel
that the students should know. Discipline is imposed from
above by the authority figure of teacher or principal, and is
enforced through fear of consequences (usually physical).

The Open School

The open school stresses freedom with responsibility.
Decisions on school administration and on curriculum are a
cooperative process involving administrators, teachers and
students. The classroom is wherever the students are--the
materials center, the community, a combination of several
classes through the use of removable walls, the individual
study carrel. Learning activities are based on the needs
and interests of the students and are highly individualized.
Planning is flexible and the "slots and bells" approach to
learning is nonexistent.

Students are responsible for completing tasks undertaken, but may move from one activity to another as the need
arises.

The materials center contains a variety of print and
nonprint media and students have free access to, and use of,
all materials in the center. Class periods are scheduled
only when a specific need arises; for example, when the
class is beginning a new unit of work and the librarian is
requested to introduce those materials which will be most
valuable for use during the unit. Small group instruction is
prevalent, with groups of students moving in and out of the

center as the need arises.   Stress is placed upon cooperation with and consideration for others and the acceptance of responsibility for one's own actions.

The Open or Closed School: A Checklist

The Open School

_____Cooperative Decision Making

_____Flexible Classroom Arrangement

_____A Variety of Learning Materials Available in the Classroom

_____Absence of Bells

_____Students Moving From One Activity to Another

_____Flexible Scheduling

_____Student Interests Determine the Learning Activity

_____Small Group and Individualized Instruction

_____A Materials Center Containing a Wide Variety of Print and Non-Print Material

_____Student Use of Nonbook Materials

_____Constant Flow of Students to the Materials Center from all Classrooms

_____Small Group or Individual Student Movement in Corridors

_____Presence of Community Leaders in the School or Students in the Community

The Closed School

_____Set Curriculum Determined by Administration

_____Arrangement of Desks in Rows

_____Reliance on Basic Text

_____Bell System

_____Students Found for the Most Part at Their Desks

_____Specific Time Slots for Each Activity

_____Curriculum Guides and the Teacher's Guide Determine
     the Learning Activity

_____Emphasis on Large Group Instruction

_____A Book-Oriented Library

_____Nonbook Materials for Teacher Use Only

_____Scheduled Library Periods

_____Entire Class Group Movement Through Corridors in
     Lines Accompanied by Teacher

_____Absence of Community Leaders in School or Visits to
     Community by Students

          Few schools will fall entirely into one rating column
or the other on the preceding checklist. In an age of educational transition it is not only possible but expected that
schools that have had a history of traditionalism will be ex-
perimenting with some progressive ideas. The checklist
should help the teacher or librarian, however, to "take the
philosophical temperature" of the school and to determine
whether the educational climate is primarily traditional or
chiefly Progressive. If the climate is for the most part
Progressive, developing an effective methods of inquiry program should not be difficult. If, however, the climate is
primarily traditional, the innovative librarian must study
those areas in which Progressive tendencies seem to domi-
nate and work through these areas to convince administrators
and teachers of the value of such a program. The process
will be slow in the predominately traditional school, but the
librarian can serve as a catalyst for change by working
through those individual teachers who show a willingness for
experimentation and desire a variety of successful learning
experiences for their students.

Surveying Faculty Thinking

It is important for the librarian to move out of the library at frequent intervals to meet with teachers on their own ground (usually defined as the faculty lounge). Through informal discussion and the display of a willingness to go the second mile in improving the educational situation, the librarian can be effective in bringing about educational change. It is necessary to know each faculty member as a person, the teaching methods and educational philosophy of each, and his individual goals for students. Certain key phrases will arise in informal conversation that will help to pinpoint the philosophy of the faculty member.

The Perennialist will frequently refer to students as "my class" rather than as individuals. His concern is with basic skills and with completing the basic text by the end of the school year. He rules with an iron hand and punishment is swift and follows the slightest infraction of laws laid down by him. His values are set and unwavering, and perfect order is the theme of his life. He is usually highly opinionated and believes in exposing children to the "classics" of literature as examples of permanencies which should best be studied. His praise is reserved for those students who apply themselves and his scorn is evident for the child who "hears a different drummer."

The Progressive teacher talks frequently of his students as individuals. He is concerned with each student's problems and development. If he uses a basic text it is used only as a guide and the material in it is not followed in rigid sequence. He encourages students to acquire information from a variety of sources and teaches through small group and individual instruction rather than large group activity. His key to instruction is flexibility but at the same time he watches each child's progress carefully. His classroom may be a jumble of materials, perhaps not too well organized to the eye of the visitor. He urges the conformist pupil to experiment and attempts to motivate the disinterested student toward greater self-realization of goals. His method of discipline is probably that of letting students suffer the consequences of their own actions. He encourages cooperation rather than competition.

The Reconstructionist and Progressive educators will have many similar qualities. Reconstructionist tendencies can be ascertained, however, in the teacher who advocates accountability and performance contracting. His concern is centered more on the outcome of the teaching-learning process than in the process itself. He is probably the first to try a new machine, new method or idea, discarding it if it does not meet the specific behavioral objectives of a particular learning situation. He firmly believes in education for social change and attempts to persuade others of his views that education must be determined by the social and cultural forces around it. He presses for changes in curriculum and materials and his classroom is a democratic one.

The Humanist teacher is easy to spot. The true Humanist lives those ideals in which he believes by placing the dignity of the human being first in all personal and educational relationships. That each individual should know his innate worth is important to the Humanist. He speaks always of his students as individuals and shows deep concern for the development of each child. He avoids criticism, ridicule, and sarcasm. His concern for learning materials is found in his attempt to place in the hands of children materials with which they will feel most comfortable and with which they are most likely to achieve. He plans almost totally for individual rather than large group instruction.

It is not unlikely that faculty members as individuals will hold views and initiate practices from two or more of the basic philosophies. A true Perennialist comes very close to being a lost cause for the Progressive school librarian but can be coaxed into allowing his students to learn how to learn, provided the initial learning activities are highly structured. Most teachers, however, will reveal chinks in the traditionalist armor and it is up to the librarian to discover these openings and work through them to help the teacher toward better methods of achieving educational goals.

A Faculty Quiz

The philosophy quiz which follows might be used at a faculty meeting or workshop to demonstrate several main points concerning the educational philosophy of faculty members. The quiz should reveal:

(1) The number of faculty members who totally embrace the Perennialist philosophy, the Progressive philosophy or a Reconstructionist philosophy.

    (2)   Those faculty members who have not yet developed a clear-cut philosophy of education.

       Of the fifteen statements on the quiz, numbers one through five reveal Progressive beliefs. Six through ten are the beliefs of the Perennialist, and eleven through fifteen are Reconstructionist views. When true responses fall within each category on a single quiz paper, it is evident that there is considerable confusion concerning a basic philosophy of education. Responses are more likely to be honest if the papers are unsigned. Group thinking can be determined quickly in this way.

       If changes in curriculum, goals, objectives, and methodology are needed in the educational process, the determination of the existing philosophies within the school is the first step in planning for change. Without a thorough understanding of the current educational climate, change is difficult, if not impossible, to bring about.

Pinpoint Your Philosophy[2]

True or False:

1. The child will learn best when motivated by his own interests.   T F

2. The process of inquiry and discovery is the best method of learning.   T F

3. Education is life as it is lived in the present.   T F

4. The teacher's role is that of guide or counselor.   T F

5. Democratic education requires the elimination of competitive practices in the classroom.   T F

6. There are certain basic truths which must be taught.   T F

7. Since man is a rational being, the school should strive to develop his rationality.   T F

8. Education is preparation for life.   T F

9. The successful student learns through hard work

and application.   T   F

10. The teacher should be an authority on subject
    matter and in matters of discipline.   T   F

11. Children's lives are shaped by the social and
    cultural aspects of the world in which they live. T   F

12. Education should strive to bring about social
    change.   T   F

13. The learning process should be based on be-
    havioral objectives.   T   F

14. The outcome of the learning process is more
    important than the process itself.   T   F

15. The most desirable social system is a demo-
    cratic one.   T   F

Defining the Role of the School Librarian

Rapid changes in school library services the past
several years have left school librarians breathless and feeling that, while the educational world in which they live is
changing at an ever-accelerated pace, they themselves are
in a state of metamorphosis.

What might finally emerge from the multi-media co-
coon is somewhat overwhelming to those who for many years
have considered themselves guardians of the print collection.
Conversely, many librarians new to the school library field
may move so quickly through the metamorphic stages that
faculty members and students will be left far behind.

New materials, equipment, methods or services at-
tempted in any library program must be accompanied by a
re-evaluation of the goals and objectives of the program and
by careful definition, which should be understood by all involved, of the role of the librarian or media specialist.
Foremost in understanding this new role must be the librarian,
for he more than any other will be the key to change.

The questionnaire which follows can be used by individual librarians to clarify their own thinking about their role
in the educational process, or can be used with administrators

and faculty members to determine current thinking concerning the role of the school librarian.

If the questionnaire is used at a librarian's meeting or a faculty meeting the answer section can be turned in unsigned and the number of A and B responses tabulated. A preponderance of either A answers or B answers will quickly reveal how ready an individual or group is for change.

If the majority of responses fall into the A group, any change in the role of the library or of the librarian lies in the far distant future, if, indeed it comes at all. All of the "A" responses define the role of the librarian as a keeper of books and a worshipper of routine. The facilities and collection are of primary importance, the students and school program are considered less important than the library itself. "A" responses clearly define the role of the librarian as an organizer and expediter of materials.

If the majority of responses fall in the "B" column, change has already taken place and more changes are on the way, based on the needs of the students served by the library. The librarian's role here is defined as that of a counselor, teacher, guide and educator, ever aware of the changing needs of students and ready to place the facilities of the instructional materials center at the disposal of students in order that those needs can be met. This role encompasses not only responding to changing needs but serving as a catalyst for change when a better method, approach or service seems indicated.

Oops! Your Theory's Showing

Directions: Complete each statement given by choosing the sentence with which you most agree. Indicate your choice in the space provided at the bottom of the page. Tear off the completed answer section. Do not sign.

1) THE SCHOOL LIBRARY
   A) is a storehouse of the world's knowledge available to all students in the school.
   B) is a place where students should develop concepts independently through the use of a wide variety of print and nonprint material.

2) IF LIBRARY FACILITIES WILL ACCOMMODATE AT
   LEAST 20% OF THE SCHOOL ENROLLMENT
   A) class and large group visits should still be scheduled
      with the librarian at least one week in advance.
   B) classes, large groups and individuals should have
      free access to library facilities without need for prior
      scheduling.

3) CIRCULATION ROUTINES
   A) should be handled by the librarian to assure careful
      charging and discharging of materials.
   B) can be adequately handled by students or volunteers
      if given proper direction.

4) IF A CLERK IS NOT AVAILABLE, THE LIBRARIAN
   A) should handle all cataloging and processing of new
      materials.
   B) should order completely processed materials when
      available.

5) WHEN A TEACHER BEGINS A NEW UNIT OF WORK
   WITH HIS OR HER CLASS
   A) the librarian should let the teacher know what ma-
      terials are available for student and teacher use
      during the study of the unit.
   B) the librarian should introduce materials to the class
      relating the materials to the concepts to be covered
      during the unit.

6) A STUDENT
   A) should always pursue purposeful activity in the
      library.
   B) should be allowed to come to the library just to
      browse or to read if he wishes.

7) THE MOST IMPORTANT JOB OF THE LIBRARIAN IS
   A) to acquire, organize and make accessible materials
      to students and teachers.
   B) to work directly with students in fostering those
      skills needed for independent study activities, and
      to help students develop a love for books and for
      learning.
****

Tear off here.   Circle your choice of answer:

1) A B   2) A B   3) A B   4) A B   5) A B   6) A B   7) A B

Summary

1. It is understood that a good school library program places a wide variety of print and non-print media at
the disposal of students, offers a large number of services
and is staffed by highly trained media personnel.

2. Within any educational complex will be found diverse philosophies of education. These might include the
philosophies of Perennialism, Progressivism, Reconstructionism, and Humanism.

3. The librarian must understand the prevailing philosophies of education found in the school for it is the philosophy that determines the curriculum, materials and method-
ology used in any educational process.

4. Developing an effective methods of inquiry program is more difficult, but not impossible, in a Perennialist
environment than in a Progressive environment.

5. Students receive as great an education outside the
walls of the school as they do within the school itself. The
school must compete with these outside educational forces if
it is to be effective.

6. Emphasis in the educational program must be
placed on learning how to learn rather than on the acquisition of basic facts.

7. The school librarian must first of all define his
own philosophy of education. Only through a clear understanding of his basic philosophy with its accompanying goals
and objectives for education can he serve as a catalyst for
change in the school.

                              Notes

1. Dewey, John. Democracy and Education. Macmillan,
    New York, 1916. p. 89.

2. Based on work done in the Pattonville School District,
    St. Louis County, Mo. by Dr. Marlin Jackoway.

Chapter 2

PREPARING FOR ACTION:
DEVELOPING POLICY

Schizophrenic Manifestations in the World of Education

Suspend belief for a moment and consider the implications for education of this make-believe world of the
1970's:

> It is a world of individual nations, each totally de-
> pendent upon its own resources for survival. Com-
> munication between these nations is cumbersome
> and slow. It is a world, however, of the printed
> page where the knowledge of mankind is duly re-
> corded for acquisition by individuals. In parts of
> this world are found fairly literate nations, al-
> though they have not yet begun to share their
> knowledge with other nations. The young of these
> nations gather in centers of education where
> knowledge can be acquired through the decoding of
> the printed page. The minds of these young are
> bombarded with facts and those who most success-
> fully complete their education are those who have
> acquired the most facts. Facts so acquired enable
> the learner to perform a specific function in an
> unchanging society.

The implications you are asked to consider for education in this make-believe world of the 1970's are obvious.
Educators have only to determine which basic facts or areas
of knowledge are to be acquired and proceed to fill children's
minds with these facts--probably through the use of basic
texts which divide all learning into subject categories and
present these desired facts in sequential order. The educational process is rational, well thought out and fairly utilitarian for the citizens of this world.

What has been described, of course, is the world of
the 19th century and early 20th century. Not only were na-

tions not dependent upon one another but individual citizens
within a single nation were fairly self-reliant. Such is not
the case today. The advent of instant technology and the
tremendous speed-up of communications have created a world
society of peoples who are greatly dependent upon one another
for survival. It has been estimated that the world's
knowledge doubles every ten years, and the instant availability and dispersion of this knowledge tends to make much
of the earlier knowledge obsolete. Yet, many educators still
insist that there are "basic areas of knowledge" which must
be acquired by students and that the best means of acquisition
of this knowledge is through one major learning tool, the
basic text, which does present facts in sequential and easily
understandable form. Thus we see one of the major schizophrenic manifestations of the modern educational scene.

The fallacy of assuming that an educated person is one
who has learned certain basic facts is best expressed by
Robert Havighurst:[1]

> As the amount of knowledge has grown so rapidly
> during the present century, we have been forced to
> give up hope that any human mind, however well
> organized, could contain all useful knowledge or
> could keep up with the growth of knowledge. There-
> fore we have been forced to change our view of the
> human mind.
>
> The human mind is now seen as an instrument for
> learning. We train the mind so that it can learn
> quickly and economically the knowledge that is im-
> portant about a particular subject. Therefore we
> train the child to use the library to look up knowl-
> edge that he needs and thus train him in the
> method of inquiry. We train for problem solving,
> for the making and testing of hypotheses. Our aim
> is to help the pupil develop a flexible and contin-
> ually learning mind.

Obviously, education does not begin or end with the
years of formal schooling. The five-year-old just entering
kindergarten has been bombarded, before he entered school,
by thousands of visual and oral experiences which enabled
him to develop manual and motor skills, attitudes, values,
interests and the skills of thinking, knowing, problem solving
and communication through the spoken word. All of these
skills have been acquired without benefit of the printed page.

Leaders in business and industry bemoan the fact that
young men and women entering the job field for the first
time have to be completely trained for the business or industry they have chosen and which has chosen them. And
yet, many teachers will insist that learning how to learn is
only incidental to the real learning process. It is performance rather than learning that is still emphasized in
many schools today. These teachers are charter members
of education's schizophrenic world, applying 19th-century educational practices to 20th-century children.

Methods of Inquiry and the Goals of Education

Once again a look at a typical school district educational policy manual will reveal that it is not the basic goals
for educating today's children which are at fault, but the
methods of achieving these goals.

A representative school district statement of policy
will read in part as follows:

We believe:

That education must provide the opportunity, in-
centive and atmosphere for each pupil to develop
mentally, physically, morally and socially to the
fullest extent of his abilities.

That education should recognize and make provision
for individual differences. The curriculum should
be so flexible as to take into consideration the en-
vironmental differences, interests, needs and
abilities of each pupil.

That a deomocratic people must of necessity be an
educated, self-disciplined people and that the ever
changing society in which we live demands that we
be able to change with it.

To write the foregoing policy costs little, but to im-
plement it is another matter. If it is understood that each
child learns as an individual (and learning is always an individual matter), then the school must provide a wide range
of services, facilities and materials to satisfy the requirements of each student within the school. If we do indeed
live in an ever-changing society, then learning how to learn

should be the primary goal of education. But this, too, is
costly for it means that education cannot be confined to a
single classroom or even to a single building, but that students must inquire, discover, and explore a large mass of
knowledge both inside and outside of the school, and must
select from this mass of knowledge that which is most pertinent to the problem at hand. The student must locate and
acquire information, determine the accuracy and authenticity
of the material, separate fact from opinion and the significant
from the less significant, determine cause and effect, evaluate his findings and reach a conclusion based on his research. The role of the basic text in this type of learning
situation is minor, if indeed it has a place at all.

Methods of Inquiry and the Development of Basic Skills

        If the student is to be guided by the teacher into the
process of discovering information independently he must be
provided with certain basic tools and skills to enable him
successfully to accomplish the task. As a primary student
in our literate society he must learn to decode the printed
page, for the printed page will continue to be, for some time
to come, one of his major sources of information. This
is not to say that the book is necessarily a permanent fixture
in our society or that knowledge is not gained even more
effectively through the use of nonbook materials, but our
present society both expects and demands literacy of its citizens. This fact should serve as salve to the wounds of the
traditionalist educator who is concerned about the acquisition
of certain basic skills on the part of students.

        As an example, examine the following list of basic
skills which a student needs to employ in most current educational institutions when he visits the school's materials
center to find an answer to a question:

   I.   He must be able to read and define and understand
        the question through the skills of:

             Word recognition;
             Word meanings;
             Comprehension.

   II. He must be able to locate the material which will
        contain the answer to his question through the em-
        ployment of locational skil's, including:

Knowledge of alphabetical order;
Knowledge of the Dewey Decimal System;
Knowing how to use the card catalog;
Interpreting information on a catalog card;
Use of call numbers to locate materials;
Knowledge of content and use of basic reference
   tools;
Knowing the parts of a book;
Knowledge of the location and utilization of non-
   print materials.

III. With the material in hand he must be able to select
only that information pertinent to the problem solving situation through employment of skills of acquisition and evaluation.

Determining main topics and subtopics;
Skimming skills;
Determining accuracy and authority;
Separating the significant from the less
   significant;
Telling fact from opinion;
Selecting main ideas;
Forming judgments;
Determining cause and effect.

IV. He must be able to communicate the information
gained through the employment of the skills of organization and recording.

Limiting the problem;
Ability to generalize;
Spelling and composition skills;
Note taking;
Ability to determine sequence;
Outlining;
Use of interesting writing or speaking style.

This brief summary of needed skills for developing
effective methods of inquiry should lay to rest any fears that
Progressive schools are expensive playrooms where no real
learning takes place.

It is important to distinguish the difference between
the pupil's need for basic facts and his need for basic skills.
Basic facts, if in truth they actually exist, are subject to
frequent change in light of new knowledge and new discover-

ies.   Basic skills are those tools which the student must
have to locate, acquire, organize, record and evaluate information.   These tools are also subject to change.   The textbook as a vehicle for imparting knowledge is obsolete.   Rote
memorization, which was considered a basic skill to be developed for many years, is no longer considered important
to the learning process.   It may well be, in the computerized
future of dial access information, that locational skills as we
know them today will also be obsolete.   In fact, there are
those who predict that the printed word will in the future be
relegated to the status of an art object, with little utilitarian
application to the acquisition of knowledge.

However, for the purposes of education in the 1970's
the printed word is still very much a part of the educational
scene, and while the student may acquire information from a
variety of carriers he will, at least for the present decade,
need to develop effective methods of inquiry if he is to move
from the basic text to multiple sources of information in the
discovery or inquiry process, regardless of the type of educational organization in the school.

Methods of Inquiry and Educational Innovation

In recognizing that learning is always an individual
process many school systems have implemented plans which
call for change in the traditional organizational patterns for
instruction, as noted on the Crossmatch Chart (page 26).
All of these patterns or programs call for a wide variety of
instructional resources and the ability of students to gain information from the resources.

The Role of the IMC

Among the most widely accepted innovative practices
are the non-graded school, team teaching instruction,
independent study programs, performance contracting, and
individualized reading programs.

Regardless of the type of organizational pattern or
teaching-learning procedures adopted by a school, the instructional materials center can play a vital part in the process provided:

1)   The IMC contains a wide variety of print and non-print
     media.

2) The materials in the center cover a wide range of reading, interest and subject levels.

3) The materials are organized for easy accessibility by students and teachers.

4) Separate areas are provided for listening and viewing activities as well as small group conference activities.

5) Space is available for large and small group instruction.

6) Provision is made for student and teacher production of materials.

7) Well trained subject specialists are available to assist students and teachers.

8) The stress of the instructional materials center program is on development of methods of inquiry.

9) Materials are introduced to students beginning a new unit of work.

10) An ongoing program of skill development is stressed.

11) The student has access to rapid information retrieval services.

12) The program stresses human resources as well as media resources.

13) Students are permitted free and unscheduled access to the IMC facilities at all times.

14) A cooperative plan of informational retrieval with other IMCs or other educational institutions is in effect.

The availability of the foregoing resources is essential to any modern educational program but does not guarantee that the program will be effective. It is accepted that the classroom teacher has more or less complete control over the educational pursuits of his or her students. It is quite possible that excellent IMC facilities might exist in a school and yet not be fully utilized, due either to teacher philosophy or to a lack of understanding by the teacher of the role of
(cont. on p. 28).

A Crossmatch Chart Relating IMC Services to Innovative Needs

A brief study of the chart below will show the importance of the instructional materials center in the school regardless of the type of educational innovation adopted by the school.

Characteristics of the Instructional Materials Center	Requirements of Innovative Practices				
	Non-Graded	Team Teaching	Indiv. Inst.	Independ. Study	Perf. Cont.
1. A wide variety of print and non-print materials	X	X	X	X	X
2. Materials on a wide range of interest and subject levels	X	X	X	X	X
3. Organized for easy accessibility by students and teachers	X	X	X	X	X
4. Listening areas	X	X	X	X	X
5. Viewing areas	X	X	X	X	X
6. Areas for large and small group instruction	X	X	X	X	X
7. Student production of materials	X	X	X	X	X
8. Teacher production of materials	X	X	X	X	X
9. Well trained subject specialists available to assist learners	X	X	X	X	X

10. Stress on developing methods of inquiry	X	X	X	X
11. Materials introduced to students on a particular study	X	X	X	X
12. Rapid information retrieval services	X	X	X	X
13. Cooperative information retrieval plan with other IMCs to provide information not available in center	X		X	X
14. Human resource file	X	X	X	X
15. Free and unscheduled access at all times	X	X	X	X

the instructional materials center in the educational process.
In order to assure efficient utilization of the IMC the teacher
must be led to an understanding of the true role of educational media in the learning situation.   Among the basic
principles to be acquired are the following:

1. In competing with the outside educational forces that
    the student meets each day (usually of a nonbook
    nature), the teacher must use new approaches and a
    variety of media to improve instruction.

2. Students learn best in different ways and by using
    those materials with which they are most comfort-
    able.   For example, a student might welcome read-
    ing a book on a screen, through the use of a micro-
    fiche reader, while the book in its original form
    may not appeal to him.

3. The teacher must know his students well enough to
    be able to determine the types of media or learning
    experiences which will be most valuable for any
    given learning situation.

4. If the use of the instructional materials center is to
    be valuable, both teachers and students must under-
    stand the particular learning goals and objectives in-
    volved in any IMC activity.

5. Teachers must develop greater expertise in gain-
    ing a wide variety of learning experiences for stu-
    dents and must become knowledgeable about cross-
    media approaches to education.

6. Media must be available on demand and the hardware
    required for the use of such media must be available
    and in good working condition at all times.

7. Both teachers and students must be familiar with
    and comfortable in using educational hardware.

8. The IMC program must undergo a process of con-
    tinuous evaluation, updating the program with new
    materials and services and eliminating those materi-
    als and services that do not prove their educational
    worth.

    The following chart indicates the application of these

principles to specific learning situations in three subject disciplines, language arts, social studies and science.

Examples of Classroom Teaching

Using the IMC	Textbook Centered
LANGUAGE ARTS	**LANGUAGE ARTS**
Students select topics of interest to them. Following a sequential pattern of development (but each proceeding at his own pace), the topic is developed through research in a variety of media culminating in a grammatically correct oral or written presentation.	Students complete workbook or textbook exercises in marking capital letters, underlining nouns, finding incorrect grammar.
SOCIAL STUDIES	**SOCIAL STUDIES**
The teacher first determines those concepts desirable for attainment by students in a particular unit of work. Using either the individual or group approach, topics are assigned for research. Responsibility for presenting information on the topic is made clear. Following the basic steps of research, the student or group uses the IMC to gather information for presentation in a variety of ways.	Students read and discuss the text, chapter by chapter, completing the exercises (usually written answers to questions) found at the end of each chapter.
SCIENCE	**SCIENCE**
The teacher first determines those concepts desirable for attainment by students in a particular unit of work. Using either the individual or group approach, topics are assigned for research. Students are urged to seek a variety of materials in finding information and may culminate the research by performing ex- (cont. on next page.)	Students read and discuss the text, chapter by chapter, completing the exercises (usually written answers to questions in workbooks or at the end of the chapter). Students watch the teacher perform experiments.

periments, presenting resource
people from the community, selecting and presenting a tape,
filmstrip or film, etc.

Preparing for Action: Establishing IMC Policies

The importance of establishing written policies for the
Instructional Materials Center program cannot be overemphasized. Written policies which establish the goals and objectives of the program, and which carefully define the program, will assure a unified understanding of the IMC center
and its services by administrators, teachers and students,
as well as by the media personnel who staff the program.
Such policies should be subject to change as the need for
change is seen, but existing policy should provide the basic
guidelines for services and use of the center and for selection and evaluation of media.

Establishing a written policy can be a difficult and
somewhat painful procedure, for it is here that variety of
philosophies of education come into focus. Several
approaches are possible. A teacher-librarian committee can
be established to develop a policy with the help and guidance
of the school or district administration. Or the IMC staff
might develop a policy for submission to an administrator-
teacher committee. In some school districts patrons also
serve on policy committees and they can make a valuable
contribution to the policy-making process, both by bringing
the parent view into the educational process and by selling
the adopted policy in which they had a part to other patrons.

Where policy does not exist, confusion reigns supreme. New media personnel coming into the school have
no clear guidelines of what is expected of them. Outdated
library practices continue out of habit even though they may
be educationally unsound. Demands are made on media
center personnel for services or materials which they may
not be equipped to supply. Or demands may be made for
services which can be supplied but which in the opinion of
the center personnel are not within the realm of their duties.
(An excellent example of this is the teacher who brings a
class to the library, expecting babysitting service while he
spends time in the lounge.)

Elements of IMC Policy

Any written policy concerning the role of the instructional materials center in the school should contain the following elements:

1. Basic goals and purposes of the IMC as it relates to the educational program in the school.

2. The organizational structure of the IMC.

3. The specific services and duties for which IMC personnel are responsible.

4. Specific programs within the school for which IMC personnel share equal responsibility with the classroom teacher (Example--Developing methods of inquiry).

5. The role of the IMC in reading guidance.

6. Services provided for teachers.

7. The scheduling or nonscheduling of classes.

8. Criteria for selection of materials.

9. Procedure for accepting complaints about materials.

10. Designation of the staff member who carries major responsibility for carrying out IMC policy and major areas of responsibility.

11. Specific guidelines for efficient utilization of the IMC by students and teachers.

12. Guidelines for cooperative programs with other libraries or educational institutions.

Policies may be established district-wide, to apply to all instructional materials centers (both elementary and secondary) within the district. Some school districts establish a district-wide materials selection policy, but establish separate elementary and secondary policies on programs and services.

The sample policies which follow were developed

following this second procedure. The policies on program
and utilization are elementary IMC policies and the selection
policy is a district-wide policy. While these policies do not
contain all of the elements previously listed they are presented here to serve as representative examples for committees working to establish IMC policies in a particular
school or district.

A note of caution. If they are to make fullest use of
IMC services, teachers must be involved in some way in the
policy making procedure. This will be a time-consuming
process involving compromise on the part of all involved,
but teachers will only make fullest use of those programs
which they completely understand and which they have had a
part in establishing.

POLICIES, PROCEDURES, AND PRACTICES
ELEMENTARY INSTRUCTIONAL
MATERIALS CENTERS
Policy Number_____
Date_____

ELEMENTARY INSTRUCTIONAL MATERIALS CENTERS[2]

I. PURPOSE OF THE ELEMENTARY MATERIALS CENTERS

   A. To assist each student in the independent acquisition
       of knowledge and in the development of concepts
       through the use of a wide variety of print and non-
       print materials.

   B. To help students grow in techniques for acquiring
       knowledge and in habits conducive to independent
       study and individual research; and to encourage
       students toward discriminating selection and use of
       a wide variety of print and nonprint materials.

   C. To aid each student in developing a love of reading
       and of books.

II. THE MATERIALS CENTER PROGRAM

   A. Organization:

       The IMC collection of materials is developed toward

goals set by ALA standards.   The collection is
well-organized and easily accessible to students and
teachers.   All print and nonprint materials are fully
cataloged by number and color-coded so that the
student can easily locate any type of material needed
for a research problem and unit of work.   Students
are encouraged to use nonprint materials when their
use will better suit a particular research purpose.
IMC quarters are maintained in an attractive manner to provide an atmosphere conducive to independent study, research, and recreational reading,
as well as listening and viewing activities.

B.   Units of Work:

Scheduling of classes for introduction of materials
related to units of work is done through teacher-
librarian cooperative planning.   The teacher must
give the librarian topics, subtopics and concepts to
be studied to assure the bringing together of pertinent materials and bibliographies for class use.
The librarian will prepare bibliographies, or guide
students in their preparation, and will gather both
print and nonprint materials for introduction to the
class, teach pertinent skills needed for use of these
materials, and conduct a class session on the topic
using tapes, filmstrips, folklore reviews, or whatever materials are necessary to stimulate interest
in the new unit of work.   She shall be available to
assist individual students at any time special help
is needed on a project throughout the study of the
unit.

C.   Teaching Methods of Inquiry:

A sequential program of teaching work/study skills
is followed in grades K-6.   Skills are always functional in nature and related directly to classroom
activity.   Broad areas of skills taught are:

Skills of Location---- Dewey Decimal System, using
                        the card catalog, alphabetizing,
                        parts of a book, knowledge of
                        basic reference books and
                        their use, location of non-
                        print materials by number
                        and color.

Skills of Acquisition– reading skills, determining
significant facts, telling fact
from fiction, selection of
main ideas, etc.

Skills of Organization– limiting a problem, ability to
generalize, note taking, out-
lining, writing a report.

Skills of Evaluation–– ability to select material appropriate to the problem,
ability to evaluate and correct
the student's finished product.

Library Citizenship–– library procedure and use,
care of books and other ma-
terials, working well in
groups, ability to work well
independently, respect for
property and rights of others.

D.   Reading Guidance:

The librarian will work cooperatively with the classroom teacher to promote interest in reading through
individual and group pupil guidance and through book
talks related to units of work. The teacher should
make the librarian aware of pupils with special
needs in order that she can get the right material
into the hands of the right child at the right time.

E.   Teacher Assistance:

The librarian shall fill all teacher requests promptly
and shall keep all faculty members informed of new
materials as they arrive. Request forms will be
placed in each teacher's box at least once weekly.
If requests are not forthcoming, the librarian shall
follow the guidance of the principal in encouraging
the use of the library by faculty members.

F.   Selection of Materials:

The elementary librarian shall be highly knowledgeable of the materials collection through wide reading
and use of the materials; shall use standard book
and media selection aids in building collections, and

shall work with principals and teachers in selection
of materials that meet curriculum needs.   Materials
shall be selected on the basis of authority, scope,
reliability, treatment, interest, format, special fea-
tures and durability.   Series of materials shall not
be purchased unless every item in the series meets
the above standards.   Materials which do not meet
the above standards shall not be accepted as gifts.
The materials purchased should assure well-balanced
collections both as to subjects and grade levels.

G.   Scheduling of Classes:

Scheduling should be flexible enough to meet the
needs of each class as those needs arise.   Every
class will be scheduled for a series of work/study
skill lessons.   Individual classes should be scheduled
frequently following teacher-librarian planning for
introduction of materials for units of work.   The
library should be available to any child at any time
that the librarian is on duty and class scheduling
should not preclude the use of library facilities by
individual students at the same time.

H.   Inventory:

Both state and federal regulations require careful
and accurate annual inventories.   A minimum of
three weeks is required at the close of the school
year to get all materials back in the library and
complete the inventory.   However, this complete
year-end inventory makes it possible for all libraries
to be ready and open for use the first day of school.
It is usually wise for the librarian to delay class
visits until she has visited each classroom and reviewed library procedure with students.   This can
easily be done in 10 or 15 minute sessions and all
classes can be seen in the first two days.   Libraries should be open and in use by all students
after the initial review of procedure.

I.   Elementary Materials Coordinator:

One elementary librarian shall be designated as
Elementary Materials Coordinator and in this ca-
pacity shall work cooperatively to assist principals
and librarians in developing the IMC program.   In

addition, the coordinator shall be responsible for
all activities of the elementary processing center
including cataloging, and supervision of processing
of materials, preparation of materials required by
elementary librarians for classwork, issuing selection lists of new materials for purchase, planning
library quarters and in-service programs, preparing
federal and state reports, maintaining all required
records for federal programs, and working with
private school personnel concerned with federal library programs.

POLICIES, PROCEDURES, AND PRACTICES
ELEMENTARY LIBRARY--
UTILIZATION OF ELEMENTARY MATERIALS
CENTERS
Policy_____
Date_____

Utilization of Elementary Materials Centers

The purpose of the elementary materials centers is to
support the teaching/learning activities of the classroom.
Elementary librarians are anxious to work with the classroom teacher in developing units of work or in providing any
supportive services to the educational program of the school.
Students are encouraged to make fullest use of the centers
in a variety of ways.

A.   In schools with flexible scheduling best utilization of the
     centers can be made when:

     1.   Students may use library facilities for individual or
          group research projects at any time the librarian is
          on duty.

     2.   Students may check out materials at any time the
          librarian is on duty.

     3.   Unit work with the entire class is scheduled follow-
          ing teacher/librarian conferences as frequently as
          the teacher desires and at a time most advantageous
          to the teacher and her class. The teacher will give
          the librarian the subject and major concepts to be
          studied during the unit and the librarian will intro-

duce materials and guide students in their use.
Teachers always accompany their class and remain
with the class during unit work to assure full integration of library activities with classroom work.

4. Class members receive instruction in basic skills.
Teachers who have been in the district more than
one year need not remain with the class during
basic skill instruction. [Four to six class periods
are needed for basic skill instruction and these
periods are usually scheduled at the beginning of
the school year.]

B. In schools where regular weekly scheduled library
periods are still necessary, best utilization of the
centers can be made when:

1. Students do small group or individual research projects during the library period. (Teachers may
want to work with students needing extra help in the
classroom during this time while other students are
receiving guidance in research by the librarian.)

2. Students select materials for recreational reading.
When members of the class come for check-outs,
students will return directly to the classroom after
selecting materials. (With the exception of those
remaining for individual research projects.)

[3. The class as a whole receives instruction in basic
skills. Teachers who have been in the district
more than one year need not remain with the class
during basic skill instruction. Four to six class
periods are usually scheduled at the beginning of the
school year.]

4. At the request of the classroom teacher, the librarian will work with the entire class in introducing
materials to be used during a unit of work. The
teacher will give the librarian the subject and major
concepts to be covered during the unit and the librarian will introduce library materials on the subject and guide students in their use. Teachers will
remain with the class during this type of library
activity to assure full integration of library activities with classroom work.

5. It is the responsibility of the classroom teacher to
    inform the librarian of the type of library period
    she desires each week, (i. e. , research projects,
    check-outs, or unit work).

	POLICIES, PROCEDURES, AND
SCHOOL DISTRICT	PRACTICES

___SCHOOL DISTRICT LIBRARIES
SELECTION OF MATERIALS
Policy Number_____
Date_____

Selection of Materials for School Libraries

  It is the premise of the School District that the school
libraries are concerned with generating understanding of
American freedoms and with the preservation of these freedoms through the development of informed and responsible
citizens.   The School Library Bill of Rights of the American
Library Association is reaffirmed.

School Library Bill of Rights
(American Association of School Librarians
-revised, 1969)

  To provide a comprehensive collection of instructional materials selected in compliance with basic
written selection principles, and to provide maximum accessibility to these materials.

  To provide materials that will support the curriculum, taking into consideration the individual's
needs, and the varied interests, abilities, socio-
economic backgrounds, and maturity levels of the
students served.

  To provide materials for teachers and students that
will encourage growth in knowledge, and that will
develop literary, cultural and aesthetic appreciation, and ethical standards.

  To provide materials which reflect the ideas and
beliefs of religious, social, political, historical,
and ethnic groups and their contribution to the

American and world heritage and culture, thereby
enabling students to develop an intellectual in-
tegrity in forming judgments.

To provide a written statement, approved by the
local Boards of Education, of the procedures for
meeting the challenge of censorship of materials
in school library media centers.

To provide qualified professional personnel to serve
teachers and students.

   The elected Board of Education shall hold professionally trained personnel responsible for the selection of all
book and non-book materials.   The selection of materials
should at all times rest with these professional people and
be consistent with the adopted criteria for selection.

A.   Criteria for Selection

   1.   The needs of administrators and teachers in relation
        to the curriculum should be of first importance.
        Since these trained persons are cognizant of the
        curriculum in the schools in which they work, any
        changes that are anticipated in offerings are dis-
        cussed well in advance so that materials shall be
        ready when needed.

   2.   Needs of the students should be of equal importance,
        based upon knowledge of children and youth.   Read-
        ing level, interest level, authorship, bias, accuracy,
        literary value, style, balance, and format will be
        considered.   It is imperative that students have all
        points of view concerning the issues of our times,
        international, national and local.   It is the responsi-
        bility of librarians to select, without bias and pre-
        judice, materials that will meet the needs of stu-
        dents.

   3.   Materials shall not be proscribed or removed from
        library shelves because of partisan or doctrinal
        disapproval.   No materials shall be excluded be-
        cause of race, nationality, political, or religious
        views of the writer.

   4.   Where possible, examination is the best method of
        selection; however, reputable, unbiased, profes-

sionally prepared selection aids should be consulted as guides. Reviews from the American Library Association, standard catalogs, learned journals in the fields of subject matter, signed reviews from newspapers, literary and educational periodicals, and other available sources can be used.

5. Gifts of materials will be accepted only if the materials offered meet the criteria set forth for selection of materials in the _____ School District.

B. Procedure for Criticism

1. Since it is the school's responsibility to provide information and enlightenment, criticism of materials that are in the libraries of the _____ School District shall be submitted to the office of the Superintendent of Schools in writing. Procedure and form _____ for this criticism shall be made in accordance with the procedure adopted by the _____ Association of School Librarians and the _____ Library Association. The procedure and form are available through the office of the principal in each school.

2. Complainant will receive written response from the Superintendent stating the action to be taken on the criticized library item.

Summary of Chapter Two

1. Many educators are attempting to teach 20th-century students with 19th-century methods.

2. The importance of learning how to learn cannot be overemphasized.

3. The development of a strong methods of inquiry program will place the educational emphasis where it ought to be today--on learning rather than on performance.

4. Basic skills which must be acquired by students for success in any independent study activity are skills of location, acquisition, organization, recording and evaluation.

5. The instructional materials center can play an

important role in the innovative educational practices of our time.

6. The IMC program will be effective only if teachers have a part in its development and have a thorough understanding of the program.

7. Written policies are needed for establishing an IMC program; including policy covering the program itself, utilization of the program by students and teachers, and selection of materials.

8. Administrators, teachers and IMC personnel should work cooperatively toward establishment of such policies.

Note

1. Brickman, William B., ed. Educational Imperatives in a Changing Culture. University of Pennsylvania Press, 1966. pp. 9-20.

2. Pattonville R-3 School District, St. Louis County, Mo. Adopted 1966. [A later version of the School Library Bill of Rights has been incorporated here.]

Chapter 3

THE REQUIREMENTS OF
A METHODS OF INQUIRY PROGRAM

The Ideal and the Alternative

It may be quite possible for the innovative librarian
to sell the administration and staff on the idea of establishing
a strong independent study or methods of inquiry program
and, indeed, to build considerable enthusiasm among the staff
for initiating such a program, only to find that enthusiasm
stops where the drain on the school district's pocketbook begins. This is particularly true in the elementary school,
where patron resistance against innovation is especially
strong. The idea of an elementary materials center is quite
foreign to many parents who did not have the advantages of
such facilities when they went to school, and who see no
real need for such "frills" for their children, especially if
the addition of the materials center means an increased tax
levy or the passage of a building bond issue. In addition,
patrons who received their education in a traditional setting
often see traditional teaching as the only approach to education. A world based on "basic facts" is still a very real
world to these parents.

Thus, the task of building such a program is formid-
able, but not impossible. A parallel might be drawn with
the young married couple who start life together with many
desires and little immediate means of achieving them. If
one is to attempt to wed the materials center to the school
program and to make the two truly one, it is necessary to
begin with the materials at hand and work slowly but con-
sistently toward well-planned goals.

There are those who fear that any attempt to start a
materials center program without at least adequate materials,
staff and facilities is doomed, that it can only produce an
abysmal status quo. Such is not the case. Small print and
nonprint collections set up in corridors or storage closets,
while far from ideal, have a way of outgrowing their bound-

aries quickly; and as collections and use of the facility grow, the demands by students and teachers for additional materials, services and space also grow. In many school districts, as these demands for better learning facilities are felt, parent groups, PTA groups, and Mothers' clubs band together with school district officials to meet the needs of the new teaching-learning program. The problem is not whether to begin such a program, but how to begin.

Staff

The most important requirement for any materials center program in the elementary school is the hiring of a trained media specialist. Unfortunately, too many school districts put the cart before the horse and, through the efforts of a zealous but misguided top administrator, manage to pass bond issues for buildings which include library facilities housing uncataloged print collections of materials and staffed by volunteer mother aides. Such facilities are often unused, for uncataloged collections make information retrieval an impossible task and schedules for teacher-student use become dependent upon the whims of volunteers. Thus a tremendous expenditure of funds has been made to do little more than promote recreational reading, a service which public library bookmobiles have been handling quite well for some time.

The media specialist will work directly with administrators and teachers to develop long- and short-range goals for the materials center program. Initial policy will be developed based upon mutually determined goals. Materials will be professionally selected to meet research needs of students and will be organized for easy accessibility by students and teachers. Applying the American Library Association's Standards for School Media Programs (ALA, 1969) to a school of 500 students, one finds that a staff of two full-time media specialists, two media technicians and two media aides is recommended. While such staffing would be highly desirable, school districts initiating a media program will frequently hire an elementary media supervisor to work with administrators, teachers and volunteers in establishing guidelines for the program and to provide the expertise in selection and organization of the materials in the collections. If this is done, the media supervisor should try to make administrators aware of the ultimate demands of the program and should develop with them long-range plans for the addition

Elementary Library Program

Expected Levels of Service
Dependent on Staff and Facilities

Staff	Levels of Service	Pupil Use
A. None	1) No library materials or service	None
	2) Classroom collections	Limited recreational reading
	3) Central print storage collection (unclassified)	Limited recreational reading
B. Volunteer Aides	1) Central storage collection (unclassified)	Recreational reading
C. Library Supervisor (district) plus Volunteer Aides	1) Setting of goals and objectives	Recreational reading
	2) Professional materials selection	Limited research activities--teacher directed
	3) Establishment of central processing--cataloged and classified collections	
D. One librarian per thousand pupils plus full time paid library aide in each school	1) Cataloged and classified collections	Wider selection of print and nonprint materials with professional guidance
	2) Limited individual and group work/study skill classes	
	3) Limited reading guidance	Limited research and reference activities
	4) Fill limited teacher requests	
E. One librarian to 500 pupils plus one full time library aide	1) Sequential skill classes all grade levels	Independent study & individually prescribed instruction

Staff	Levels of Service	Pupil Use
(clerk takes care of charging materials & routine clerical tasks, releasing librarian's time for professional duties listed in column 2)	2) Full time assistance to groups and individual students on research & reference	Discriminating selection of materials
	3) Teacher/librarian planning for introduction of materials for units of work	Acquisition of a broad range of work/study skills
	4) Guidance in listening & viewing activities	Individual & group research
	5) Meet all teacher requests	Clearer understanding of concepts through having materials introduced for units of work
	6) Preparation of bibliographies	
	7) Classes in literature appreciation	
	8) Full time assistance to individuals & groups in reading guidance	Becomes familiar with a wide variety of print & non-print materials in his search for information
	9) Assistance to faculty in curriculum planning & selection or professional materials	
		Gains greater appreciation of books & reading
		Improved academic skills
F. One full time librarian One media aide One media technician	All of foregoing in Level E plus graphics production & display, photographic production, tape production services, equipment operation and maintenance	All of foregoing plus development of slide, tape, transparency programs. Development of graphic displays, film production.

of staff, materials and space. In addition, the media supervisor will develop a plan of action based on present materials, staff and facilities, and will develop guidelines for the
use of established centers.

A major pitfall in the development of a media program is to attempt to provide too many services in order to
"sell" the value of the program to administrators, teachers,
students and parents.   Limited materials, facilities and staff
must also mean limited services. As the center grows, and
staff members and materials are added, services can be expanded. It is a major function of the media supervisor to
determine what services can be offered and to insure that
they are of the highest possible quality.

The chart on pages 44 and 45 shows the relationship
of the media center's staff to the type of services that can
be provided, assuming a basic collection of materials exists.

Materials

If students are to develop a wide range of concepts
independently through the use of a variety of materials, these
materials must be readily available and easily accessible.
Once again, long-range planning is essential to provide direction for the development of the materials collection and
guidelines for use of the materials.

Using the hypothetical elementary school of 500 students as a model, the ALA Standards calls for a basic collection of 10, 000 books, a minimum of 40 periodicals and three
newspapers, 1, 500 filmstrips, 3, 000 recordings, 500 8mm
films and access to 3, 000 16mm film titles, as well as a
variety of pamphlets, clippings and miscellaneous materials.
In working toward this goal it is important that nonprint materials be added simultaneously with print materials and that
the collections grow together toward ultimate goals.

It is essential in any methods of inquiry program to
do away with the idea that print sources are the "best"
sources of information--a common idea in our literate society.   Print sources alone will not develop listening skills
or visual experiences and have little value for the nonreader.
If the school is truly to provide for individual differences
and for the needs of all students, the filmstrip or the record
are equal in importance to the book.   For the student read-

ing below grade level, there is no stigma attached to the
filmstrip or the recording, and it is discovery itself rather
than the means of discovery that is important.

In building the materials collection many administrators feel that classroom collections should be broken up
and housed centrally to provide the nucleus of the center's
collection. This is usually an unwise practice for the
following reasons:

A. Teachers tend to become quite attached to books
    purchased over the years with PTA or other funds.
    Having housed these materials in their rooms for
    some time, they do not wish to part with them and,
    when forced to do so, will develop a negative atti-
    tude toward the use of the media center.

B. Most classroom collections are outdated and in poor
    condition, and the major portion of materials will
    prove to be of little value in the materials center.

C. The idea that the teacher will no longer have a
    classroom collection of books must be replaced by
    the idea that the classroom will always have a large
    collection of materials borrowed from the central
    collection. These materials will be ever-changing,
    depending upon the demands of the curriculum. If
    teachers are to accept this idea, they must actually
    experience the use of the IMC in the school.

A Basic Materials Collection

While these figures are by no means ideal, it is
possible to initiate a methods of inquiry program in a school
of 500 students with the following basic collection (collections
for larger schools would be proportionately higher): Books:
3500-4000; Periodicals: 20 titles; Filmstrips: 300-400; Newspapers: 2 (1 national, 1 local); Recordings--Disc & Tape:
300-400. Transparencies, study prints, pamphlets, clippings
and miscellaneous materials will prove helpful also if they
can be added in any amount.

Balancing the Collection

As materials are added to the collection it is im-

portant to maintain a balance within various subject categories to avoid too heavy an emphasis in one area at the
expense of another area of the curriculum. Maintaining
such a balance will help to assure the availability of materials in all curriculum areas as demand arises. A bal-
anced collection helps to prevent the tendency on the part of
the librarian to meet only specified requests, when there
may be other needs which are not verbally expressed but for
which there is a demand. A suggested balance for both print
and nonprint collections in the elementary school is as
follows:

000	5%	600	6%
100	1%	700	4%
200	1%	800	4%
300	6%	900	20% (incl. biography)
400	2%	Fiction	20%
500	12%	Easy Books	20%

Building the Collection

An initial expenditure of $20.00 per pupil for two
years will establish a collection of approximately 3,200
books, 300 records, 300 filmstrips, 20 periodicals, two
newspapers and some miscellaneous items. Subsequent ex-
penditures of $10.00 per pupil per year will insure fairly
rapid growth of the collection. The commitment of funds
from PTA groups and from federal programs will further
aid the growth of the materials collection.

The chart which follows shows the growth which can
take place over a five-year period, based on a commitment
of $20.00 per year for the first two years and $10.00 per
year per pupil for the next three years. Film loops and
16mm films are not included in the budget since in building
an initial collection three filmstrips can be purchased for the
cost of one loop, and it seems wisest to build up the filmstrip collection first. Most schools cannot afford to purchase
16mm films, and either rent films or belong to a film cooperative, paying an annual fee for film service.

Requirements of a Program

First Year
  (500 pupils @ $20.00
   per pupil)

1500 Books	7500.00
200 Recordings	1000.00
200 Filmstrips	1200.00
20 Periodicals	120.00
Misc.	180.00

Second Year
  (500 pupils @ $20.00
   per pupil)

1700 Books	8500.00
100 Recordings	500.00
100 Filmstrips	600.00
20 Periodicals	120.00
Misc.	280.00

Third Year
  (500 pupils @ $10.00
   per pupil)

700 Books	3500.00
100 Recordings	500.00
100 Filmstrips	600.00
20 Periodicals	120.00
Misc.	280.00

Fourth Year and Fifth Year
  (500 pupils @ $10.00
   per pupil)

800 Books	4000.00
50 Recordings	250.00
50 Filmstrips	300.00
30 Periodicals	180.00
Misc.	270.00

To Catalog or Not to Catalog?

While it may seem illogical to the trained media specialist or librarian, a very common stumbling block in the development of the IMC program is the administrator who sees no need for classified and cataloged materials in the elementary school. If policy and goals are written and accepted early in the program, however, this should not be a problem. How, indeed, can the student become proficient in the development of methods of inquiry if he is not able to retrieve the material he needs quickly and easily--the primary purpose of cataloging and classification! And if the student is to become equally proficient in the use of print and nonprint materials, then all materials must be cataloged for easy accessibility. It is a truism that the amount of time and effort placed on input (in cataloging and classification) is directly related to the amount of time the student must spend on output (gaining accessibility to the materials). This is not to say that the time of the media specialist should be spent in typing catalog cards or even in cataloging materials. If the school is understaffed with media personnel, as is most likely the case, then priorities must be placed on the time of the media specialist; and if developing methods of inquiry is the primary goal of the program, the time of the librarian should be spent with students and teachers in this pursuit. This, of course, means provision either

for district-wide centralized processing or for purchasing
fully processed materials.

Space Requirements

        One of the most pressing requirements in the ele-
mentary school is the need for space. The materials center
program, often the newest program to be added, must compete with established programs in music, art, physical education, counseling, speech therapy, instrumental music and
remedial reading for operating space in the school. For the
ideal center in an elementary school of less than 1, 000
pupils, the ALA Standards calls for space approximately equal
in size to the area of eight to ten classrooms. Again, if
the ideal cannot be met, the media specialist must strive for
a practical alternative.

        In the City of St. Louis, where many of the older
school buildings have wide halls, the idea of corridor libraries has been developed. Attractive reading, study and
browsing areas have been established in these hallways, adjacent to classrooms. In other school districts, cafeterias
have been developed into materials centers; these usually
provide more space for a variety of activities than a con-
ventional-sized classroom. This, however, is possible only
in older buildings where cafeterias and gymnasiums are
separate and are not built as multi-purpose rooms. It must
be emphasized that these are far from ideal media center
facilities; however, many worthwhile programs have grown
from small beginnings.

        In most school districts, the initial IMC program is
established primarily in one classroom, with space for only
a very small collection and which will not provide for the
variety of listening, viewing and research activities necessary in a methods of inquiry program. If, however, one
classroom is all of the space that can be provided at the
outset (long-range plans having been made for the addition
of larger facilities), then fullest use of this space must be
made. This can be done in several ways.

    A.   The Use of Rotating Collections.

        The librarian must work closely with classroom
        teachers to provide classroom collections which are
        changed frequently to meet the demands of the cur-

riculum.   In addition, a wide range of reference
materials must be provided in the IMC to assure
supplementary research facilities for students. The
reference collection should include both print and
nonprint materials.

B.   Satellite Centers.

Primary collections can be established in corridors
adjacent to primary classrooms, providing easy
accessibility to materials by kindergarten through
grade two students.   Student aides can be assigned
to keep these collections in order and circulation of
materials can be very informal.   Primary teachers
needing materials for a unit of work can notify the
librarian, who will see that these particular materials are gathered from the center and sent to
the classroom.
        If the school is departmentalized, collections
within the department subject area can be housed
in or near the department.   A complete record of
the location of these materials should be kept in
the materials center.

C.   Learning Packages.

Learning packages of print and nonprint materials
for frequently requested subjects can be developed
by the materials specialist for loan to classrooms
or groups of students researching a particular topic.
These packages can be cataloged and stored in areas
other than the center itself as long as they are
easily accessible.

Block Scheduling

        In a true methods of inquiry program pupils should
be allowed to make fullest use of the materials center whenever the need arises.   Thus, rigid scheduling should be
avoided at all costs.   Scheduling of classes may be necessary and desirable when a class is beginning a particular
unit of work, so that the librarian can introduce students to
the materials likely to be of help to them during the study
of the unit.   Teachers may also request that a class be
scheduled if the need for teaching skills is evident.   How-

ever, the use of the center by an entire class should not
preclude its use by individual students seeking information.

It is obvious that one classroom of space cannot
accommodate even one-fifth of the students in the school at
any one time. While block scheduling is not a highly desirable solution, it may be necessary to initiate it until additional space becomes available.

Use of Microfiche

Inexpensive microfiche readers are now available at
a cost that does not prohibit their placement in most elementary classrooms. Hundreds of fiction and non-fiction books
for the elementary school are available on microfiche for
one-sixth to one-half the cost of the hard copy, and over 100
full-length books on microfiche can be stored in the space
taken by one conventional book. Where space is a problem,
the extended use of microfiche for student research activities
provides an excellent alternative.

Combining Space Saving Plans

All of the foregoing space-saving ideas can be used in
combination to provide for maximum use of available space.
The key to effective space utilization is careful planning.
This, in turn, requires close cooperation with the teaching
staff to determine the most pressing needs for media center
use and to develop use patterns which will meet those needs.

Retraining the Administration and Faculty

It is a generally held belief that the principal (more
or less) determines the learning atmosphere of the school
and that faculty members (more or less) have fairly complete
control over the whereabouts of their students--including
whether or not those students make use (or misuse) of the
media center in the school.

Newly trained media personnel find to their amaze-
ment that the presence of even the finest facilities and materials, in the form of an up-to-date materials center, does
not guarantee the center's use. Reasons for the lack of use
of the media center by students and teachers may be many;

among them, a lack of materials or space, or reluctance on the part of media personnel to be of service. However, assuming a large, well stocked center with willing media personnel to assist students and teachers, if little use is still being made of facilities, the major reasons are likely to be: a) classroom teacher ignorance concerning the vital role of the IMC in the instructional processes, and b) teacher resistance to innovation.

Keeping in mind the reasons for scheduling an entire class group in the library or materials center, study the Check List for Evaluation of an Elementary Library Class Period which follows:

Check List for Evaluation of an
Elementary Library Class Period

Introduction: A successful elementary library program is fully integrated with the curriculum of the school. Students work independently and in groups to strengthen existing concepts and to build new concepts through discriminating selection and use of a wide variety of materials. Skills of acquisition, location, organization, recording, and evaluation are strengthened through functional use of library facilities. In observing a good library program, the following points should be noted: (Six or more yes answers indicate an excellent program.)

		Yes	No
1.	Teacher-librarian cooperative planning precedes the class visit to the library		
2.	The library class session was arranged to meet specific needs of the class		
3.	There is evidence of careful preparation of the lesson by the librarian		
4.	There is evidence of preparation of the class for the visit by the teacher so that students know the purpose of the visit and can take an active part in the lesson to be presented		
5.	A tape, filmstrip, story, or recording presented by the librarian correlates directly with classroom work		
6.	Provision is made for functional use of any skill or skills taught		
7.	The librarian has good control of the group and handles discipline problems effectively		

54   Developing Methods of Inquiry

<table>
<tr><td></td><td></td><td>Yes</td><td>No</td></tr>
<tr><td>8.</td><td>The librarian's lesson presentation is clear and opportunity is provided for discussion and questions from the group</td><td></td><td></td></tr>
<tr><td>9.</td><td>Materials presented cover an appropriate range of grade levels to provide for individual difference</td><td></td><td></td></tr>
<tr><td>10.</td><td>In subsequent library visits, students utilize the materials and skills presented in independent learning activities guided by the classroom teacher and librarian</td><td></td><td></td></tr>
<tr><td>11.</td><td>Where space permits, students from other classes are working independently in listening, viewing or research activities, or are locating materials at the same time the class is in session</td><td></td><td></td></tr>
</table>

All of the activities listed presuppose an ultimate independence of use of the media center by the pupil which must be taught. The emphasis is on a functional approach to the acquisition of skills developed through the cooperative endeavors of the teacher and librarian. To assume that the classroom teacher is capable of assisting students in developing skills for independent study is a mistake. Recent research studies indicate that most classroom teachers cannot make efficient use of materials centers and do not have a thorough understanding of the skills involved in developing efficient methods of inquiry.

In an interesting study with obvious implications for school libraries, Perkins tested 4,170 college seniors in teacher education institutions in 38 states, checking their competence on tests designed to measure familiarity with libraries.[1] The institutions included some which might be assumed to produce primarily elementary school teachers (State Teachers College, Dickinson, North Dakota) and others which probably include a sizeable proportion of prospective secondary school teachers (Bucknell University). The primary finding of this study was that "no evidence was gained from these tests to contradict the hypothesis that prospective teachers, as a group, cannot make intelligent use of library facilities."[2]

In a speech delivered at the AASL Membership Meeting during the ALA Conference in St. Louis, Missouri, on June 30, 1964, Dr. Paul W. F. Witt of Columbia University

stressed this lack of teacher familiarity with instructional
materials and library use.   Dr. Witt emphasized that there
was no well-defined plan in most teacher-education institutions for preparing teachers to use and select instructional
materials and to utilize the resources and services of school
libraries.   "Research and experimentation in teacher education, particularly that conducted by the more influential
teacher educators, " he said, "has rarely been focused on
problems involved in teaching teachers to be understanding
and skillful users of materials. "[3]

    Often found in combination with this lack of knowledge
is a resistance on the part of administrators and teachers to
innovation of any kind.   A teacher may resist accepting a
new role in which he does not feel confident, or utilizing
hardware with which he is not familiar, or perhaps simply
because he feels that the present state of the teaching art is
sufficient and he can see no good reason to change his teaching practices.   It is necessary, therefore, to define carefully the role of the administrator and teacher in the methods
of inquiry program, and to work toward the retraining of the
staff so that each will feel confident of his capability to
carry out his part in a successful methods of inquiry program.

The Role of the Principal

    The major role of the school principal in relation to
the instructional materials center is to be fully aware of it
and its program.   While this may sound obvious, many librarians bemoan the fact that the principal neither knows nor
cares about what goes on in the media center as long as he
is not disturbed.   It is the primary obligation of the elementary school principal to use every means possible to improve the instructional program in his school.   This includes
a complete understanding of the role the instructional materials center is to play in the educational program, the
goals and objectives of the media program, the activities of
students and teachers as they relate to the use of the center,
and the role of the librarian in providing the necessary
services and meeting the demands of students and teachers.
It is the obligation of the principal to examine and support
justifiable requests for the upgrading of materials, facilities
and staff of the media center.   It is the principal's obligation to encourage new or reluctant faculty members to make
fuller use of the facilities and to be able to discuss intelli-

gently with patron groups the role of the media center in the
school.

Helping the Principal Toward Awareness

One means of helping the principal to become aware
of the role of the IMC and of the media personnel in the
school is through evaluation. Most school administrators are
required to submit written evaluations to the district superintendent on each member of the instructional staff, either
semi-annually or annually. Unfortunately, most districts use
a single evaluative form for all instructional personnel, and
the basic criteria for evaluation are related chiefly to the
role of the classroom teacher. Since the role of the media
specialist is much broader than the classroom teacher's, a
separate evaluative form should be developed which will more
accurately define the role of the media specialist for the
principal and give him a greater understanding of the instructional materials center's function in the school. A
sample list of criteria items for evaluation might read as
follows:

1. THE LIBRARIAN AS A VITAL PART
   OF THE LEARNING PROGRAM:

   A. Understanding and implementation of the
      goals of the IMC program as they relate
      to the total educational program of the
      school.

   B. Familiarity with the course of study K-6
      and with the instructional materials suited
      to the course of study and the needs of
      students.

   C. Understanding and application of child
      growth principles and development.

   D. Cooperation with faculty members in de-
      veloping and implementing units of work
      and in selecting, locating and introducing
      materials to students.

   E. Prompt attention to faculty and student
      requests.

F. Professional competence in the selection and acquisition of materials.

G. Maintenance of the materials collection in a well organized manner to assure easy accessibility of materials to students and teachers.

H. Planning learning situations in accord with accepted principles of learning.

I. Maintains student order and discipline to assure an IMC environment conducive to learning.

J. Operates effectively within school district policies.

2. THE LIBRARIAN AS A MEMBER OF THE FACULTY AND PROFESSION:

A. Contribution to the total school program.

B. Contribution to good school morale.

C. Active cooperation with school personnel.

D. Personal characteristics related to teaching.

E. Membership in professional library organizations.

3. GENERAL ESTIMATE OF LIBRARIAN.

This list of criteria items, used in conjunction with the checklist for Evaluation of an Elementary Library Class Period given earlier, should help the principal gain a better understanding of the role of the IMC in the school, especially if these items are supplemented by oral and verbal reports by the librarian on both the progress and the problems of the program.

Defining the Role of the Classroom Teacher

Moving from an instructional program in a self-contained classroom to the development by students of methods of inquiry through research and discovery is no easy task.

An independent study program requires a complete re-thinking
of the teaching-learning process on the part of the teacher.
It means that if the basic text is used at all, the teacher
uses it only as a springboard or guide to the wealth of information available on any particular subject. The teacher
must assume the role of guide and counselor to help students
develop the skills of location, acquisition, organization, recording and evaluation of material to develop concepts independently.   More work will be done with small groups and
individuals and less time spent in large group situations.
The teacher must become familiar with the wide variety of
materials that students will be using, and must be able, along
with the librarian, to help students find those materials with
which they can work most comfortably.   In summary, the
classroom teacher must know his students, the curriculum,
and the methods and materials involved in the development of
independent study programs.

Re-Training the Classroom Teacher

        A number of approaches can be taken in helping the
teacher toward a better understanding of the materials center
program as it relates to the learning process.   No matter
what approaches are selected, it is important to realize that
the teacher is a trained professional and that, while he may
lack specific knowledge in one field, his expertise in the
teaching process and his knowledge of child growth and development should be utilized in cooperative planning sessions.
If media personnel assume a superior or condescending attitude toward the teacher, the learning process will stop before it has begun.   Tact, helpfulness and cooperation are the
bywords for media personnel in working with the classroom
teacher.   The teacher's knowledge of his student's needs and
of the demands of the curriculum, combined with the librarian's knowledge of material, can provide for a successful
learning environment if both agree upon and follow through
with similar methods for the development of methods of inquiry.   Thus, personal contact is one of the most valuable
means of helping teachers to see the value of the IMC program.

Personal Contact

        A willingness to assist the teacher should be evident,
but there should be no hint of any attempt by the librarian

to tell the teacher how to teach.   Tactful suggestions for improvement of instruction may be made, but with care and only after a firm cooperative relationship has been established.   Prompt attention to teacher requests can be a vital factor in selling the services of the center to the teacher. The librarian who knows what is being taught in the classroom can meet demands before they are made, by making available to the teacher newly received materials which might prove helpful.   Teacher requests for new materials should be encouraged and met as soon as possible.   Of primary importance is assistance to students, so that they return to the classroom feeling pleased that their search for knowledge has been successful.   Media personnel should make every effort to get out of the library to visit classrooms, to be aware of what is going on in the school, and to visit informally in the lounge with teachers to become more fully aware of their problems and needs.

Service Forms

        While it is not possible to see every teacher every day, it is still possible to help alert teachers to the services of the media center through the use of service forms placed in teachers' mailboxes several times weekly.   If the forms are given out en masse once yearly, they are often filed and forgotten.   A frequent distribution will help remind teachers of the center's services and of the willingness of the staff to be of assistance.   In using the form below, or a similar form, a word of caution is necessary.   The teacher should not have to fill out a form for every request.   The forms serve only as a reminder, not as a necessary piece of paperwork to be taken care of before a request can be filled.

ELEMENTARY LIBRARY PROGRAM

Request for Service

Teacher_____

1.   Introduce materials for a unit of work: Date____Time__
      Name of Unit_____
      During the introduction, please stress_____

2. I am sending a group of children for research and reference activity: Date_____Time_____

    Please have reference materials available on _____

    Set up:____listening center____filmstrip viewers
    ____tape recorder   ____record player

3. Schedule work/study skill class: Date____Time_____

4. Schedule a story hour: (Note: story hours must be related to units of work.) Story should have as its main topic or theme: _____Date____Time_____

5. Other request:_____
    _____

6. Send the following materials to my classroom: (list on reverse side)

Bulletins

         The use of bulletins by the media center staff can be of invaluable assistance in stimulating faculty-student use of the IMC.   These bulletins may be concerned with new materials that have arrived in the center, new programs or services that have been initiated, changes in programs or procedures, or simply news bulletins concerning the activities of the center.   The sample bulletin which follows has as its purpose the introduction of IMC services of which the teacher may not be aware.   It is as important in bulletins as it is in personal contact to avoid criticism or preaching-- hence the humorous tone of the sample bulletin.

Elementary Library Bulletin

HAVE YOU CAUGHT THE LIBRARY BUG?????????

         Rumor has it that this bug has been very active lately.   Many faculty members who have caught the bug report that once the system has acquired it, it is practically impossible to throw off.   (Rumor also has it that the elementary librarians are in "cahoots" with leading drug manufacturers to see that no cure for the bug is ever found!) Quiz yourself and find out if you have caught the bug.

1. When I begin a new unit of work I make it a
    point to see the librarian and arrange a time
    for my class to visit the library as a group.
    The librarian will introduce the materials that
    my students will be using to build broad new
    concepts.

2. I make the librarian aware of my students who
    need special help in selecting reading materials
    on their level, so that these boys and girls
    can enjoy reading and can be able to contribute
    to class discussions in all areas of work.

3. Whenever the librarian is on duty I send stu-
    dents to the library to work on individual re-
    search projects related to units of work. My
    students are most enthusiastic about being al-
    lowed to seek knowledge independently.

4. I take advantage of the special help the librar-
    ian is willing to give to my primary students
    in doing simple research projects. I fre-
    quently send a small group of first or second
    graders to the library to discover the answer
    to a question and report back to the class.

5. I frequently send pupils to the library to pre-
    view filmstrips and tape recordings that they
    then present to the class.

6. I continually turn in requests for materials
    that I want to see ordered for the central li-
    brary.

7. I spend a good deal of time in the library be-
    coming aware of the wide variety of materials
    that are available for units of study. I plan
    my units with these materials in mind.

IF YOU CAN ANSWER YES TO SIX OUT OF THE
SEVEN STATEMENTS THERE IS NO DOUBT AT
ALL: YOU HAVE CAUGHT THE LIBRARY BUG!

Questionnaires

   The use of an evaluative questionnaire with teachers can have a twofold benefit. First, the results of the questionnaire can point out the strengths and weaknesses of the IMC program and help media personnel develop new directions for service. Second, and perhaps more important, the questionnaire is designed to help teachers extend their thinking concerning their goals for students as they relate to the library services offered.

   Considerable experience in the use of the questionnaire has revealed some typical results. If it is used with a teaching staff which has had two years or less experience in using the IMC, the majority of teachers will list as their major goal for students using the materials center, "to develop a greater love of reading and of books." Teachers who have worked in a strong methods of inquiry program for three years or more will state that their major goal for students is to "develop concepts independently through use of a wide variety of materials." These teachers will also indicate that they see the major role of the librarian as supervising and assisting students in individual research activities, while the less experienced teacher sees the major role of the librarian as "helping students in the selection of reading materials." In other words, the process of moving teachers from a self-contained classroom, basic text approach to teaching to fullest utilization of the media center will take approximately three to five years. When the majority of the staff is working successfully in the program, the new teacher is encouraged to work into the program more quickly and the process of re-training is a shorter one.

INSTRUCTIONAL MATERIALS CENTER QUESTIONNAIRE

New State Standards for Accreditation will require elementary libraries in the schools of the State for the first time beginning with the coming school year. We have tried to develop an elementary library program based on the best practices in library services recommended by the American Library Association. However, we are always concerned with improving the program to provide those services that will most help you in reaching your goals for students and to aid each student in reaching his full educational growth. We would appreciate your answers to the following questions. It is not necessary to sign this questionnaire.

1. School_____

2. Which of the following goals do you feel is most important for your students to reach in using the materials centers this year? Check two.

   a. Develop concepts independently through use of a wide variety of materials.
   b. Develop proficiency in working alone.
   c. Develop greater discrimination in selection of materials.
   d. Develop a greater love of reading and books.
   e. Become independent in use of audio-visual materials.
   f. Become more proficient in note taking, outlining and organization of material.
   g. Improve listening and viewing skills.
   h. Other_____

3. In which of the following ways are library services most helpful to you in reaching your goals for students? Check two.

   a. Materials sent to classrooms on teacher request.
   b. Materials introduced to classes centered around units of work. .
   c. Work/study skill classes.
   d. Helping students in selection of reading materials.
   e. Helping students in selection and use of audio-visual materials.
   f. Supervising and assisting students in individual research activities.
   g. Assisting small groups of students or individual students in research activities.
   h. Book talks related to units of work.
   i. Other_____

4. In what way do you feel the use of library facilities would be most helpful to your students?

   a. Library facilities available to any child at any time the librarian is on duty, (for group or individual work or selection of materials by small groups of individuals.)
   b. Classes scheduled at any time the teacher requests to work on particular skills or present materials for units of work.
   c. A combination of A and B.

    d. One regularly scheduled weekly class visit.
    e. Other_____

Please add any other comments on this sheet that would
help us in improving the library program.

In-Service Programs

       In-service programs can be an effective means of
teacher training if two conditions are met. The programs
must be well planned, with specific learning objectives, and
they must be held at a time when the teaching staff is most
likely to be receptive to new ideas. This means that the in-
service programs must be related to the specific media center program that teachers are expected to follow, rather than
based on general theories of learning. The training sessions
must allow for teacher participation, whether in the operation
of specific types of equipment or in the development of a
functional program of methods of inquiry. Provision should
be made for teachers to undertake those activities which they
will be initiating with students, to assure a complete understanding of the process. Finally, released time from the
classroom should be provided for in-service programs. When
such programs are held at the end of the school day or in
the evening, the teacher, tired from a busy schedule, cannot
bring his best to the learning situation and will take away
little in the way of new ideas. The programs should be di-
rected only by someone who has a complete understanding of
the materials center's role as it applies in the development
of methods of inquiry within a particular school district. In
a word, the in-service program should be as practical as
possible. The outline of such a program follows:

Developing Methods of Inquiry
An In-Service Program for Teachers

Effective Utilization of Instructional Materials
or
Getting the Most Out of Your School's IMC

A full day workshop covering the following topics:

I. Defining Terms*

   A. The Instructional Materials Center

      A place where students support or deny existing concepts and develop new concepts independently through the use of a wide variety of print and nonprint materials.

   B. Teaching

      Guiding children to discover concepts independently. Helping children to acquire the skills necessary for the successful pursuit of knowledge. Caring deeply about the development of each individual child according to his needs and abilities.

   C. Learning

      That which occurs every waking moment in the life of a human being. The most successful learning experiences are those marked by flexibility, the use of a wide variety of resources, and based on the interests of the learner.

II. The Role of Media in the Instructional Process

   A. Learning Activities and the IMC.   An Overview
      1. Listening Activities*
      2. Viewing Activities*
      3. Fostering Creativity through Media*
      4. Independent Study Activities

III. The Research Process - A Functional Approach

   A. Skills needed for the Independent Pursuit of Knowledge
      1. Skills of Location
      2. Skills of Acquisition
      3. Skills of Organization
      4. Skills of Recording
      5. Skills of Evaluation

   B. Guiding the Research Process
      1. Structured Activities*
      2. Unstructured Activities*

IV. The IMC and Reading Guidance

    A. Helping Children Through Books

    B. Guiding the Discussion

    C. Books which may help students to meet the developmental goals of childhood. (Specific titles to consider)

*Active participation of workshop participants

    In addition to the in-service training offered by the school district, many colleges and universities will offer courses in effective use of the media center if sufficient enrollment for such a course is obtained. Such courses can often be taken for graduate credit and, while they are based on general concepts rather than a district's specific program, they can be very helpful in acquainting teachers with the variety of media available and in introducing new ideas on the use of these materials. Such courses are highly recommended.

Summary

    1. While it is not always possible to begin a methods of inquiry program under ideal conditions, a start should be made using present facilities in the school and working toward the improvement of these facilities through the development of long-range plans.

    2. The most important requirement for any materials center program in the elementary school is the hiring of a trained media specialist or librarian.

    3. The number of services that can be provided in any media center is directly dependent upon the staff and facilities of the center.

    4. Long-range plans should be developed for the acquisition of a balanced collection of print and nonprint materials using the requirements of the ALA Standards for School Media Programs as an ultimate goal.

    5. A cataloged and classified collection of materials

is essential to a methods of inquiry program.

6.   Every effort should be made to utilize all existing space in the school for the media center program, including the use of rotating collections, satellite centers, learning packages, block scheduling and the use of microfiche.

7.   Ignorance as to the vital role of the IMC in the instructional process and resistance to innovation are major reasons for the lack of teacher use of facilities.

8.   The chief means of helping the principal to become aware of the role of the IMC in the school is through developing evaluative procedures which require his active participation.

9.   A successful methods of inquiry program requires the cooperative efforts of the classroom teacher and the librarian.

10.   Classroom teachers can be made aware of the role of the IMC in the teaching-learning process through personal contact, service forms, bulletins, questionnaires and in-service programs.

Notes

1.   Ralph Perkins, The Prospective Teacher's Knowledge of Library Fundamentals; A Study of The Responses Made by 4,107 College Seniors to Tests Designed to Measure Familiarity with Libraries (Scarecrow Press, 1965).

2.   Ibid., p. 193.

3.   Dr. Paul W. F. Witt, "Teacher Education and School Libraries," School Libraries, XIV, No. 1 (October, 1964), 37-46.

Chapter 4

THE FIRST STEP: READING GUIDANCE

The Teaching of Reading: A Major Function

An extremely large portion of the primary student's
school day is devoted to the process of learning to read. As
students progress up the educational ladder the percentage of
time allocated to this activity decreases somewhat, but by the
sixth grade it still remains as a major activity. Those
who disagree with these statements overlook the enormous
amount of time spent in the upper grades on the definition of
terms in the various subject disciplines. In our literate society, this heavy emphasis on reading skills and vocabulary
building in the elementary school is an accepted way of life,
for regardless of background, opportunity, mental ability,
motivation, emotional stability and a host of other factors
which make each child a unique individual, every child is expected not only to learn to read but to learn to read well.

In the past, schools have justified their efforts in the
development of reading skills by citing input factors; that is,
the number of teachers, the qualifications of the teaching
staff, the amount of time in the school day devoted to the
reading process, and the amount of money spent on reading
materials and library resources. In our new era of accountability and performance contracting, these factors are no
longer considered relevant. It is not the method but the result with which society is now concerned, and in the case of
many students the results have not been spectacular.

The reasons for failure of many reading programs are
three-fold: 1) the emphasis on developing reading skills
rather than readers; 2) conforming to society's demands for
"doing away with (or not adding) frills"; 3) overlooking the
basic need of each child to find his place in the sun.

68

Emphasis on Reading Skills

A survey taken recently in a midwestern elementary school asked teachers to define the word "reader" as it applies to an individual. The question was stated as follows:

A student is considered a reader when_____.

Among the responses were these:

1) A student is considered a reader when he has a good basic sight vocabulary, understands phonics and uses phonetic analysis in attacking new words.

2) A student is considered a reader when he has successfully completed the basal reading program of the elementary school and understands and applies the skills he has learned to his reading ability.

3) A student is considered a reader when he has learned the basic reading skills and uses these skills in independent reading activity.

4) A student is considered a reader when he hides Henry Huggins or Homer Price inside his math book.

If this same survey were taken in most of the nation's elementary schools it is likely that the majority of responses would define a reader by the number of basic skills he has acquired. Only the last response above really comes close to differentiating between having the ability to read and being a reader.

The teacher who made this response actually defined a reader as one who prefers to read over most other activities, as one who finds great joy or pleasure in the reading activity. It is precisely this aspect of reading that is so often overlooked in elementary classrooms. The development of basic reading skills is considered by many the end of reading instruction rather than the means of developing a love of reading and of books by today's students.

Parents tend to equate their own educational experiences with those of their youngsters, and regard any new material or method with suspicion. Thus, films, filmstrips, recordings, reading machines, microfiche readers, overhead projectors, listening centers and even school libraries are looked upon as either "nice to have but not really necessary," or as "a waste of the taxpayer's money." The conformity of every child to an arbitrary standard in educational achievement was expected twenty years ago and most parents feel it should still be expected today. This idea of conformity is extended to include the materials used by students, and the idea of providing each student with the type of material with which he will best achieve is looked upon as "mollycoddling." Thus, efforts to try new approaches or to obtain funds for new programs or materials are often met with failure, and many teachers who might otherwise be innovative in their approach to individualizing instruction, give up in frustration.

If every child could be helped to develop a positive self-image and to feel confidence and success in the learning situation few remedial problems would exist in the schools. A case in point if that of John _____. John had always been a Robin.

Even in first grade John knew what this meant. The Bluebirds were the kids who learned the system early and achieved well. The Robins were the class "dummies." Even by the time he had reached fifth grade, where reading groups were no longer labeled, John knew that he was still a Robin. By fifth grade, however, the problem was compounded, for even though John was given a basal reader that his achievement scores indicated he could handle, he was also given the same science and social studies textbooks as every other child in the classroom, and was expected to learn from them.

John had compensated for his difficulty in learning to read by learning to "aud." It is possible to see words but not be able to read. It is also possible to hear sounds but not to comprehend what is heard. Thus, "auding" is to hearing as reading is to seeing. John's teacher quickly noticed his ability to learn from oral experiences and, being a wise teacher and a humanist, she helped John to capitalize on this ability.

During a unit on the Civil War, class groups were to report on various aspects of the war. Following a teacher/librarian conference on John's difficulties, time was provided for John to listen to the Landmark Recording, We Were There When Grant Met Lee at Appomattox. This recording mentions quite a number of Union and Confederate Generals. As John listened he followed a list of the Generals' names and noted those who fought on each side of the conflict.   In presenting the recording to the class, John told the students to listen carefully, since he had some questions for them at the conclusion of the record.   Following the listening experience John asked one question: He said, "It's pretty important to know who the leaders were in the Civil War if we are going to talk about it.   When I say these guys' names I want you to tell me which ones was from the north and which ones was from the south. "   The blank looks which met him as he called off most of the names helped John to find his place in the sun.   For the first time in his entire school career, John knew something that the rest of the class didn't know!

Perhaps this activity did not help John to become a better reader, but it did provide him with a positive learning experience which helped him achieve a better self-image.   If John and many other students like him (who have given up because they have met little but failure in the learning experience) can be helped to find pleasure in learning, they can be led to the self-realization of the many doors to learning that reading can open for them.

Media Personnel and Reading Guidance

The librarian or media specialist has a unique role to play in the school in helping children to develop a love of reading and of books.   Students are neither required or expected to "give anything back" to the librarian as far as the learning process is concerned.   The librarian does not make value judgments or issue grades.   Thus media personnel are in a unique position in the school to listen to, to attempt to understand, to help, to encourage and to show sincere interest in every child with whom they have contact.   And contact is the key to reading guidance.   Two examples should suffice to make this point.

Librarian A (or media specialist A, if you prefer) can be found at the circulation desk almost any time one visits the library.   She is a walking card catalog and is happy to pause from her timeless task of taking care of the return materials and issuing new materials to students, to direct boys and girls to the shelf which will contain the particular item they seek.   Her remarks to students consist chiefly of directions such as, "you will find dinosaur books in the science stacks, middle section, second shelf from the bottom!" She makes sure that the media center is well organized at all

times and that materials are easily accessible to students and
teachers. She knows the collection well but becomes slightly
exasperated when she is required to repeat directions to for-
getful students.

·   Librarian B (or media specialist B) is almost never
found at the circulation desk. Her attitude goes something
like this: "Why should I waste my time stamping those idiot
cards when the kids can do it themselves? Lost books?
Sure, we have a few snags but what is more important, a
lost book or a youngster who needs help?" She is especially
aware of the student she has not seen in the center for a few
days and makes it a point to give a special greeting to these
students, taking time out to chat with them about their activities. On occasion the materials center has been noted to be
"a bit of a mess." However, the student asking for a dinosaur book is not only taken to the shelves where the book is
to be found, but is helped to choose the best book for his
purpose. Browsing is encouraged and students are slightly
awed and quite impressed at Librarian B's knowledge, not
only of the location but of the content of the materials. Students like to be around this librarian for she makes it clear
through her actions that their needs are important and that
she understands that one child's needs will be different from
those of another.

Why Reading Guidance in an Audio-Visual World?

          The chief source of most of our students' knowledge is
not the classroom but the television set. For information
and entertainment, this medium is superior to all others, in
the judgment of most students. Why then should we attempt
to develop a love of reading and of books, except as a source
of information which the television may not be immediately
able to supply? The value of the reading experience lies in
its individuality. Audio-visual experiences are usually shared
experiences, and while they may have great value, they are
not as highly personalized as the reading experience.

          The book is a highly portable medium requiring no
additional hardware or software for its use. To the reader,
the delight and enjoyment found in a good story is endless.
Other books on a similar subject or theme or other books by
the same author are always available. The vicarious experiences provided by literature can be lived again and again.
An examination of the motives which lead characters to

specific acts in books can help students gain greater insight
into their own lives.   The reading experience can provide a
means of quiet escape from a world with too many pressures
or worries, and in some instances can help a student to
think out his problems.   What child has never felt like Harriet in Louise Fitzhugh's Harriet the Spy, who keeps a notebook filled with comments about friends and enemies alike--
comments she would like to make but which conformity to
society prevents her from making except in the privacy of
her notebook?   What child doesn't recognize himself or others
in the fiendish children portrayed in Roald Dahl's Charlie and
the Chocolate Factory?   What delight there is in seeing the
horrible children in this book come to a disastrous but de-
served end!

The reading experience stretches the imagination and
can lead children to create their own literary worlds.   The
style of a favorite author may be copied initially, but as the
young writer's confidence grows his own style will emerge.
Our next generation of writers can only come from our present generation of readers.

Media Center Activities for
Fostering the Reading Experience

1.   Reading Aloud to Children

The child who has little difficulty in learning to read
is the child who has been read to from infancy.   The family
sharing of good books from an early age makes the reading
experience an accepted part of daily life, and habits established early in life are difficult to break.   Children who have not
shared a series of humorous or exciting stories with parents,
brothers and sisters, but who have only been given a steady
diet of television, will see little value in learning to read.
Unfortunately, in our fast paced society, the sharing of literature in a family has become more and more a rare experience.

Both teachers and media personnel, then, must be prepared to share literature with children and to introduce boys
and girls to the pleasures to be found in the world of books.
Several studies have shown that most teachers do not undertake a great deal of personal reading.   The average number
of books read for pleasure by public school teachers as a
group ranges from three to five a year.   While the teacher's

amount of personal reading may seem to be his or her own
business, additional studies have shown a direct correlation
between the amount of personal reading done by a teacher and
the amount of reading done by the students of that teacher.
In other words, enthusiasm is catching, and children are
quick to see the sham of a pretended enthusiasm.

        Students should be read to each day, regardless of
their grade level.   The literary experience can be enjoyed by
any age if the choice of literature is appropriate and if it is
read with true enjoyment and enthusiasm.   Because they are
more comfortable with the tried and true, many classroom
teachers are reluctant to try new books with students; having
once completed a course in Children's Literature, they have
not read a new children's book since.   If the media specialist
is to help promote reading in the school, he faces a two-fold
job.

        First, he must read, read, read!   He must know
children's books and be able to recommend them with knowledge and enthusiasm to students and teachers.   He must keep
teachers up-to-date on the best of the new and persuade them
to widen their reading horizons.   This can be done by issuing
annotated lists of new books to teachers, by bringing new
books into book talks when presenting material to a class for
a unit of work, and by personal notes accompanying books to
teachers, giving reasons why a particular book might be especially suitable for a class.

        Second, the media specialist must know the students
he serves, providing open access to all materials, and never
denying a child a book he chooses simply because it may be
too difficult for him.   If the librarian is to bring children
and books together on a one-to-one basis, he must know the
personal interests of the children as well as the content of
the books.

2.   Stimulate Reading Through Audio-Visual Experiences

        The book is not a natural medium with many children.
For those children who have had difficulty in learning to read,
it is both a distasteful and uncomfortable medium.   No
amount of enthusiasm about the contents of a book will encourage them to try it if they don't have to, for the book, to
these children, represents failure.

In the primary grades, audio-visual experiences in the field of literature may help to prevent this initial failure by leading the child to reading through those experiences which he associates with pleasure.

The assumption is made in most primary classrooms that children enter the first grade unable to recognize the printed word. The teacher might be surprised if, instead of writing on the board, "Dick and Jane," she wrote Ajax, Prell and Gleem. From years of experience in watching television, 95% of first grade students will recognize those words, along with Mattel, Alka Seltzer and Kleenex, and a host of others. The words have been added to the child's sight vocabulary from seeing them on a screen and hearing them pronounced at the same time. The listening center can prove a valuable extension of this familiar experience. The teacher can request of the media center staff that stories be recorded on cassettes at a slow enough pace to enable children to follow the printed word in a book. Many excellent children's books have been commercially done in this manner and provide a far more enjoyable reading experience than filling in blanks on workbook pages.

One fear of the primary teacher which can be quickly set to rest is the concern with controlled vocabulary. This fear centers around the idea that because the vocabulary in Curious George or Choo Choo, or whatever book is being used with the listening center, is not the same as that presented in the basal reader, the student may not recognize the words and will become discouraged in the reading experience. Most first graders have little difficulty with large words. They enjoy the story of Choo Choo, even with its vocabulary extended to include words like brake, locomotive, and engineer. It is not the large words which give first graders trouble. It is more likely to be words like "from," "with," and "was," over which they stumble. The listening/reading experience will reinforce the use of these words.

Any commercial recording used with children should be previewed before purchase. This may be the job of the media specialist or a combined effort of teachers and media personnel, but if the goal is to stimulate the desire to read, then the literary experiences must be of the very best. One area which requires the most careful previewing before purchase is the "classics." One example of a poorly done classic is a recording of Black Beauty produced by a well-known record company. In this version of Anna Sewell's famous story, the

record begins with a loud neigh from "mother horse" as she
proceeds to give saccharin advice to Black Beauty. Later in
the recording, when Beauty stops in a storm and refuses to
cross a bridge, the coachman proceeds to have a long-winded
conversation with the man on the other side of the bridge
which reveals the fact that there is no bridge. Most first
graders (for whom the story was never intended) are wonder-
ing by this time why the horse is so much smarter than the
man! While every item should be previewed, the Spoken
Arts Literature series and the Newbery Award recordings
produced by Miller-Brody Productions are generally excellent
reproductions of children's classics.

Almost all elementary children feel comfortable with
viewing experiences. This feeling can be capitalized on
through the use of filmstrips or microfiche. In the case of
filmstrips used in individual viewers, the reading experience
may be limited, but because the captions help to explain each
frame, students will usually read them. For older children
there is no stigma attached to a filmstrip. It is a personal
viewing experience and one which children enjoy.

Microfiche, for the elementary school, is a relatively
new medium. Over one thousand children's books suitable
for grades 1-8 are now available on microfiche. Once again,
because of the familiarity of the screen, students will frequently read a book on microfiche which they refuse to read
in its hardback form. School districts which have initiated
the use of microfiche report that unexpected results have occurred during the first year of the microfiche program.
Students who have viewed a book on microfiche subsequently
ask for the book in its hard-cover form and apparently re-
read it and share it with others. In a like manner, students
who have seen a film of a particular book, whether at school,
on television or at the movies, often wish to secure and read
the book.

3.   The Story Hour

One of the best means of helping children to find
pleasure in the reading experience is the story hour. To be
effective, however, it requires considerable preparation on
the part of the librarian. While many excellent children's
stories are available on sound filmstrips, these are best reserved for use in the classroom, for they require little preparation other than the simple mechanical operation of equipment.

The successful story hour in the media center requires the librarian to be not only a book enthusiast and a child psychologist in the selection of exactly the right book for each group, but a thespian as well. There is nothing quite so enjoyable as a well-told story. The secret of the storyteller's art lies in being able to communicate directly with those who are listening. As the storyteller speaks, he watches his audience and interacts with them. If the children appear amused he allows time for laughter, and constantly plays upon the mood of the group, changing it at will as the story demands.

In selecting material for the story hour the storyteller must choose a selection that he enjoys. He does not memorize the story, but reads it over a number of times until it becomes thoroughly familiar to him. He should attempt to tell the story aloud before presenting it to a group, to discover if there are areas which need re-reading to gain greater familiarity. Occasionally, the story may be more effectively presented through the use of visual aids such as the flannel board, shadow pictures, or transparencies. Following the story, items of interest might be examined, as for example, arrowheads following an Indian story.

The media specialist most in demand for storyhours is one who also has a working knowledge of the guitar. Stories told in song are always popular with children. Most first graders enjoy joining in on the chorus of The Fox Went Out on a Chilly Night and can spend hours pouring over Peter Spier's very detailed drawings in this marvelous book.

4. Non-Fiction Book Talks

The enthusiastic media specialist can do a great deal to broaden children's reading interests through non-fiction book talks. All children, regardless of grade level, have special interests and natural curiosity. The opportunity to introduce books of non-fiction to a class should never be missed. Once again, the use of concrete objects to bring the books alive should be considered. The success of one elementary librarian, who has specialized in non-fiction book talks, is attributed not only to her enthusiasm concerning the books but to her use of such objects. In introducing books on insects to first graders a box of meal worms went along as standard equipment. A bird unit in the second grade saw a robin's egg passed from child to child without damage. Another second grade studying amphibians and reptiles was

treated to the feeding of two frogs on the floor in the middle
of the classroom.   Artifacts from the Cahokia Indian Mounds
were examined by sixth grade students beginning a unit on
archeology, and great care was taken to see that all objects
used were discussed in some detail in the books presented.

The reading interests of remedial students are often
limited and for this reason they tend to enjoy non-fiction
more than fiction.   First and second graders enjoy science
books, particularly those on reptiles and prehistoric life.
Third and fourth grade boys keep the automobile shelf empty,
while the girls are finding cookbooks and sewing books. Fifth
and sixth grade girls are not as avid non-fiction readers as
the boys, whose interests lie in sports heroes in general and
hockey and football in particular.   Every elementary library
should provide ample materials in these areas to prevent
students having to wait for materials.   The remedial student
is difficult to motivate and once motivation has been achieved,
a wait for materials will prove discouraging.

5.   The Use of Paperbacks

Most teachers and media personnel will agree that the
paperback book has far more appeal to children and adults
alike than its hardback counterpart, perhaps because it
doesn't seem like a "real" book because of its reduced size
and portability.   Libraries have numerous ways of handling
paperbacks.   Some have paperbacks for sale only, others
handle paperbacks just as they do hardback material, cataloging and circulating them in the same way.   Still other libraries maintain large paperback collections that are neither
cataloged nor provided with book cards.   For developing the
desire to read, this latter method has been most successful.

An initial purchase of three books per student will establish the nucleus of a paperback collection.   This is considered to be an expendable collection that will need to be
replaced annually, so no cataloging is done nor are the books
provided with pockets or cards.   Instead, each student is
given a book which he chooses from the collection.   He may
keep his book or trade it in at any time for another.   If he
has paperbacks at home which are suitable for the collection
he may either donate or trade these.   The student is not required to sign out his book and no circulation records are
kept.   It is a completely free book exchange plan with no red
tape involved.

Objections which have been raised to this plan are obvious. The book in its hardback form does not have to be
replaced annually while the paperback does. However, the
paperback collection is intended to be a supplement, not a
substitute for the hardback collection, and at current prices,
an annual expenditure of one dollar and a half a year per
child is all that is required to stimulate reading interests
and to develop the desire to read on the part of many students who would not otherwise be motivated. A great deal
more than this is spent in the schools on remedial programs
which might in part be prevented through the wider use of
paperbacks.

Developing the Literature of Children

Elementary children should be given every opportunity
to develop their natural creativity. It was stated earlier that
the reading experience can lead children to create their own
literary worlds. Both the materials and facilities of the
media center are ideal for developing these creative writing
activities. A step-by-step program for developing creative
writing experiences can be successfully followed through the
use of study prints and uncaptioned filmstrips.

Use of Study Prints

Many companies produce study prints designed to present a single concept or piece of information on a particular
topic. The prints are large and colorful and the reverse side
of the print usually gives information about the picture. A
fifth grade teacher used three of the prints from the Instructional Aids Set Number 9 on Groundwater. She displayed
the prints and asked students to write one sentence telling
what the picture reminded them of. The first print was of
the stalagmites and stalactites in the Lily Pad Room at
Onondaga Caverns in Missouri. Comments were as follows:

1) I wonder what the outside looks like?

2) shoestrings hanging out of a wall

3) a haunted house with secret passages

4) a batch of candle drippings

5) a snow mountain with icicles

6) a place where cavemen hung their spears

7) someone's brain with jaggedy things hanging from it

The second print was of Riverside Geyser in Yellowstone National Park. Students' written comments were:

1) a bull's nostrils when he is about to charge

2) a dragon leaping through the mist

3) an upside down Christmas tree

4) a genie coming out of a bottle

The third print is more difficult to describe. It is three petrified trees which form a triangle surrounded by almost barren sloping land in Yellowstone National Park in Wyoming. Students said this picture reminded them of:

1) three tombstones in a sunken living room

2) a graveyard with rocks as rough as sandpaper

3) where Frankenstein rose from the dead

4) a place where ghosts walk over your body

5) the sight of it makes me want to inhale

6) three men in distress, slowly but surely being suffocated by quicksand

7) the shape of the trees and their bark form a mouth which is open in a loud burst of scream for help

Following the initial descriptions, students were encouraged to extend their sentences into short paragraphs using descriptive words and passages.

Uncaptioned Filmstrips

Many companies produce sound filmstrips which are
uncaptioned. While these are generally used with sound for
the pure enjoyment of the story, they can also be used without sound, or perhaps with soft background music to set the
mood, for creative writing activities. For a real challenge
a filmstrip without a definite storyline is best. A beautiful
filmstrip to use for this purpose is the Weston Woods Production of Wheel on the Chimney by Margaret Wise Brown
and Tibor Gergely. It is the story of the migration and
world travels of a group of storks who return each year at
nesting time to the wheel on the chimney. Following the
viewing of the strip, a second grader wrote this story:

> Some storks were flying south. There was a stork
> gathering grass to make a nest. The storks flew
> in bunches. One of the storks fell on a ship. A
> captain gave it food and later it flew away. Then
> summer came again. The stork built another nest
> in someone's tree. They saw the nest and they
> were happy.

In using uncaptioned filmstrips for creative writing, care
should be taken to see that the sound filmstrip is not presented at a later date. Children will frequently ask if they
"got the story right" and need to be reassured that the story
they wrote is the right story for them and that there is no
right or wrong when they are creating their own stories.

The final step in the creative writing activity is writing a story without the use of visual aids. This does not
mean, however, that the writing activity is unmotivated.
Students' original stories might be placed in the materials
center for others to read or they might be presented to another class. One fourth grade was asked to write Halloween
stories to present to the primary grades and one youngster
did such an outstanding job that his teacher encouraged him
to illustrate the story for presentation. The illustrations
were then put on transparencies. The happy ending to this
activity was that this student had not achieved exceptionally
well in other areas and the students in the class openly
showed their pride in his accomplishment. His story, which
follows, was both original and clever:

The Witch

There once was a witch who was a very mean witch
indeed. She had a magic ring which made her quite
powerful. In fact, the ring made her so powerful
that she could change human beings into any kind of
animal at all.

The witch had a butler who was a very nice man.
She made him work very hard for her. He knew
that if he could get the ring away from her she
would be completely powerless. It seemed an impossible task. However, the butler was very sad
and did not enjoy working for the witch. He had to
do difficult chores for her and all kinds of strange
things. One day the butler had an idea. When he
brought her her supper he said he dropped his dime
and asked her to pick it up. When she was bend-
ing over to pick it up the butler hit her over the
head with a tray. He was not sure she was dead
so . . . .

He grabbed the ring, put it on his own finger and
changed her into a pig. She squealed and squeaked
and finally ran out of the room. He knew that the
witch could never bother him again because she was
merely a pig. Also he had the magic ring. But
since he was such a kind-hearted and good man he
had no use for that ring.

The butler was so happy about being really free for
the first time in his life that he was going to make
sure that the magic ring was destroyed so no one
else could ever use it to do evil. He tossed it
into the fire and watched it melt and set out to find
himself a job in a nice,
                                normal,
                                        home!

Books to Read Aloud

Without the ability to decode the written word, students will make little progress in school, will become quickly
discouraged, and will label themselves as failures in any
learning situation involving reading. While it is true that all
children will not progress in reading at the same rate, the

the great majority of students can learn to read well enough
to function in society.   The goal in the elementary school,
however, should be far greater than the simple teaching of
reading skills.   Developing a love of reading runs a close
parallel to developing a love of learning and fostering a spirit
of inquiry.   Through learning to enjoy the written word
children can be led to the development of their own literature,
which they should be encouraged to share with others.

No one approach to reading will work with every child.
The basal reader will serve as the vehicle for teaching reading skills to most, while audio-visual materials may prove to
be stepping stones to reading for others.   But, regardless of
the approach or material used, enthusiasm on the part of
both teacher and media specialist in knowing and presenting
the best in children's literature can greatly stimulate the desire to read.   The list which follows contains both newer and
older books that children especially enjoy having read aloud
to them.

READ ALOUD BOOKS

Kindergarten

Barrett, Judi, Animals Should Definitely Not Wear Clothing.
    Atheneum, 1970.
    Describes the problems which animals might face if
    they had to wear clothes

Brunhoff, Jean de. Story of Babar.   Random, 1933.
    An elephant leaves the jungle to live in Paris.

Burton, Virginia.   Mike Mulligan and His Steam Shovel.
    Houghton-Mifflin, 1939.
    Mike and his beloved steam shovel dig the cellar of the
    new town hall.

Elkin, Benjamin.   Six Foolish Fishermen.   Hale, 1958.
    Six brothers go fishing and children participate in trying
    to find the lost brother.

Fatio, Louise.   The Happy Lion.   Whittlesey, 1954.
    A lion's cage is left unlocked and the lion decides to
    visit the town.

Flack, Marjorie.   The Story about Ping.   Viking, 1933.

A chinese duck who stays out all night to avoid a spanking.

Gramatky, Hardie. Little Toot. Putnam, 1939.
A tugboat learns the ways of New York Harbor.

Keats, Ezra Jack. Hi, Cat! Macmillan, 1971.
A neighborhood show put on by Peter and his friends is interrupted by a cat.

Nodset, Joan L. Who Took the Farmer's Hat? Harper, 1963.
Each animal who sees the lost hat interprets it as a different object.

Piper, Watty. Little Engine That Could. Platt, 1954.
A little engine carrying Christmas toys has difficulty getting over a mountain.

Rey, Hans. Curious George. Houghton-Mifflin, 1941.
A monkey's adventures in the city and the difficulties he encounters.

Sendak, Maurice. Where the Wild Things Are. Harper, 1963.
A little boy sent to bed without dinner dreams of wild creatures.

First Grade

Alan, Sandy, The Plaid Peacock. Pantheon, 1965.
A peacock saves Scottish soldiers from a brush fire.

Aliki. Keep Your Mouth Closed, Dear. Dial, 1966.
A crocodile swallows everything in sight.

Freeman, Don. Corduroy. Viking, 1968.
The story of the adventures of a department store bear.

Freeman, Don. Mop Top. Viking, 1955.
A little boy who avoids haircuts until a lady offers to buy his hair for a mop.

Hoban, Russell. A Bargain for Frances. Harper, 1970.
Frances, the badger, learns a lesson in economics.

Kantrowitz, Mildred. Maxie. Parents, 1970.
An old lady who lives in an apartment feels alone and
unwanted until all the neighbors come to investigate when
they do not see her one morning.

Littell, Robert. Gaston's Ghastly Green Thumb. Cowles,
1970.
A little boy who can't keep his thumb out of his food
finds that a vegetable garden begins to grow from it.

Lobel, Arnold. Frog and Toad Are Friends. Harper, 1970.
Five short stories in an easy to read book about friendship.

McCloskey, Robert. Blueberries for Sal. Viking, 1948.
A human mother and a mother bear lose their offspring
when they go berry picking.

Miles, Miska. Fox and the Fire. Little, 1966.
Realistic story of a fox and a forest fire.

Regniers, Beatrice Schenk de. May I Bring a Friend:
Atheneum, 1964.
A little boy brings animals to the king's party.

Sauer, Julia L. Mike's House. Viking, 1954.
A little lost boy explains that Mike's house is the
library where his favorite book character lives.

Seuss, Dr. The Lorax. Random, 1971.
A lesson in ecology told in an amusing manner.

Second Grade

Armour, Richard. · Animals on the Ceiling. McGraw-Hill,
1966.
A story poem about a little boy with a vivid imagination.

Battles, Edith. The Terrible Trick or Treat. Addison-
Wesley, 1970.
The difficulties of a small boy on trick or treat night.

Berg, Jean Horton. Miss Tessie Tate. Westminister, 1967.
An unconventional lady takes up skating for a hobby which
proves useful.

Bulla, Clyde Robert. Valentine Cat. Crowell, 1959.
A princess, a chimney sweep and an artist tell the story
of the valentine cat.

Cass, Joan. The Cats Go to Market. Abelard, 1970.
The amusing story of the battle of a fish seller to get
rid of the cats.

DuBois, William Pene. Lazy Tommy Pumpkinhead. Harper,
1966.
The difficulties of a young boy in an electronic world.

Freeman, Don. Hattie the Backstage Bat. Viking, 1970.
The story of a bat who lives in a theatre and accidently
gets in the limelight.

Hurd, Edith Thatcher. Catfish. Viking, 1970.
A cops and robbers story involving the fastest cat in
town.

Kahl, Virginia. The Perfect Pancake. Scribner, 1960.
The town's best cook is tricked by a beggar into making
many pancakes.

Lifton, Betty. Joji and the Dragon. Morrow, 1957.
A scarecrow saves a farm from destruction by a Japa-
nese dragon.

Low, Alice. Herbert's Treasure. Putnam, 1971.
Herbert collects odds and ends from the dump to the
displeasure of his mother.

Monjo, F. N. Pirates in Panama. Simon & Schuster, 1970.
Brother John saves the church's golden altar when pirates
burn the city.

Payne, Emily. Katy No Pocket. Houghton, 1944.
Katy has no pocket to carry her son and being a kang-
aroo, sets out to find a pocket.

Peet, Bill. Farewell to Shady Glade. Houghton, 1966.
Animals must find a new home when civilization takes
over the forest.

Ward, Lynn. The Biggest Bear. Houghton, 1952.
A boy's problems with a bear cub that grows into adult-
hood.

Warner, Gertrude. The Boxcar Children. Whitman, 1950.
Four orphan children who live in a boxcar.

Grade Three

Bulla, Clyde, Robert. White Bird. Crowell, 1966.
An orphan boy who has been kept hidden from the world
by Luke who wants to protect him goes into the world
in search of his white crow.

Caudill, Rebecca. Did You Carry the Flag Today, Charlie?
Holt, Rinehart & Winston, 1966.
Charlie is finally awarded the coveted honor of carrying
the flag in school.

Cleary, Beverly. The Mouse and the Motorcycle. Morrow,
1965.
The adventure of a mouse named Ralph who finds a toy.

Corbett, Scott. The Disappearing Dog Trick. Little, 1963.
A city roundup of stray dogs finds Waldo without his
license.

Dahl, Roald. The Magic Finger. Harper, 1966.
A little girl has her way when she points her finger at
others.

DeJong, Meindert. A Horse Came Running. Macmillan,
1970.
A midwestern tornado brings troubles and a stray horse
to a young boy who must cope with both.

Farjeon, Eleanor. Mr. Garden. Walck, 1966.
Mr. Garden appears and brings life to the garden. In
the fall he disappears.

Mason, Miriam. Susahanna, the Pioneer Cow. Macmillan,
1941.
The Wayne family and their animals travel from the
Virginias to the midwest by covered wagon.

Mosel, Arlene. Tikki, Tikki, Tembo. Holt, Rinehart &
Winston, 1968.
The story of the reason Chinese give their children
short names.

88   Developing Methods of Inquiry

Panetta, George.   A Kitchen Is Not a Tree.   Norton, 1970.
A little boy attempts to raise a baby bird in an apartment.

Peet, Bill.   The Wump World.   Houghton, 1970.
An ecology story of the invasion of the Wump World by
creatures from the planet Pollutus.

Place, Marian.   The Resident Witch.   Washburn, 1970.
A young witch who can appear as a real child becomes
the star attraction at an amusement park.

Sayers, Frances Clarke.   Oscar Lincoln Busby Stokes.
Harcourt, 1970.
The story of a little boy's problems over his nickname.

White, E. B.   Charlotte's Web.   Harper, 1952.
The story of Charlotte, the spider who saves her friend
Wilber, the pig from the fall slaughtering.

Wilder, Laura Ingalls.   Little House in the Big Woods.
Harper, 1953.
The life of the Ingalls family in the 19th century.

Fourth Grade

Angelo, Valenti.   The Tale of a Donkey.   Viking, 1966.
A mistreated donkey escapes and finds a new life with
an Italian boy.

Atwater, Richard.   Mr. Popper's Penguins.   Little, 1938.
The problem of keeping a penguin as a pet.

Butterworth, Oliver.   The Enormous Egg.   Little, 1956.
A hen hatches a dinosaur egg.

Cleaver, Bill and Vera.   Ellen Grae.   Lippincott, 1967.
Ellen, who has a history of telling tall tales, is not
believed when she tells the truth.

Cushman, Jerome.   Tom B. and the Joyful Noise.   West-
minster, 1970.
A black boy growing up in New Orleans must reconcile
his love for jazz with the disapproval of his grandmother
with whom he lives.

Dahl, Roald. Charlie and the Chocolate Factory. Knopf,
1964.
The story of five children who meet with disastrous
consequences on a tour of a chocolate factory.

DuBois, William Pene. Porko Von Popbutton. Harper, 1969.
A fat boy finds his weight an asset in a school hockey
game.

Gee, Maurine H. Flood Hazard. Morrow, 1966.
The heroism of a boy who meets the challenge of a flood.

Gray, Nicholas. Over the Hills to Fabylon. Hawthorne,
1970.
A prince of reason, a nervous king and a disappearing
kingdom are elements in this story of fun.

MacKellar, William. A Ghost Around the House. McKay,
1970.
Jasper invites a ghost to live in his house. The ghost
interferes with Jasper's father's paintings and trouble
begins.

Malot, Hector. Remi. Hawthorn, 1970.
A French boy sold to a traveling showman by his foster
father seeks his real identity.

Michel-Dansac, Monique. Peronnique. Atheneum, 1970.
A simple boy in the days of knighthood recovers a
sacred lance and cup.

Selden, George. A Cricket in Times Square. Ariel, 1960.
A cricket, mouse and cat are friends at a Times Square
newsstand.

Turkle, Burton. Mooncoin Castle. Viking, 1970.
A jackdaw and a ghost attempt to prevent their castle
from being torn down to make way for a shopping center.

Fifth Grade

Armer, Alberta. Trouble Maker. World, 1966.
A troubled young boy who has difficulty adjusting to a
foster home.

Bradbury, Bianca. The Loner. Houghton, 1970.

A boy who feels he cannot compete with his older brother
finds confidence in a summer job.

Burnford, Sheila. The Incredible Journey. Little, 1961.
Three animals travel together facing hunger and danger
on a 2500 mile trip.

Cleaver, Bill and Vera. Grover. Lippincott, 1970.
A boy's adjustment to the death of his mother.

DeJong, Meindert. House of Sixty Fathers. Harper, 1956.
A Chinese boy caught behind enemy lines during World
War II survives through his own wit and courage.

Fleischman, Sid. Chancy and the Grand Rascal. Little,
1966.
A boy and his uncle outwit a scoundrel and capture a
band of outlaws.

Forbes, Esther. Johnny Tremain. Houghton, 1953.
Set in the Revolutionary War period this is the story of
an orphan who attempts to prove his identity.

Gates, Doris. The Cat and Mrs. Cary. Viking, 1962.
A story of Mrs. Cary, a talking cat, ghosts and
smugglers.

Gipson, Fred. Old Yeller. Harper, 1956.
A Texas boy left in charge of his family in 1860 encounters difficulties.

Levitin, Sonia. Journey to America. Atheneum, 1970.
The trials of a Jewish family fleeing from Hitler's
Germany.

Lippincott, Joseph. Wilderness Champion. Lippincott, 1944.
A puppy becomes the leader of a wolf pack.

O'Dell, Scott. Island of the Blue Dolphins. Houghton, 1960.
The story of an Indian girl who survived alone on an
island for 18 years.

Sixth Grade

Burch, Robert. Queenie Peavy. Viking, 1966.
A young girl rebels when her father is sent to prison.

Byars, Betsy. The Summer of the Swans. Viking, 1970.
The story of a teen-age girl and her 10-year-old re-
tarded brother.

Catherall, Arthur. Antlers of the King Moose. Dutton,
1970.
The tracking of a king moose by experienced hunters.

Cleaver, Bill and Vera. Where the Lilies Bloom. Lippincott, 1969.
A family kept together by a 14-year-old girl after the
death of their father.

Day, Veronique. Landslide. Coward, 1963.
Five children are caught in a landslide and buried in a
cottage.

Fitzhugh, Louise. Harriet the Spy. Harper, 1964.
Harriet loses her notebook in which she has recorded
personal thoughts about friends.

Garfield, Leon. Smith. Pantheon, 1967.
The story of an 18th century London pickpocket.

Hamilton, Virginia. The House of Dies Drear. Macmillan,
1968.
A strange house bought by a new family provides danger
and excitement.

Lipsyte, Joseph. The Contender. Harper, 1967.
A Negro boy's struggle to become a prizefighter.

Merrill, Jean. The Pushcart War. Scott, 1964.
Pushcart vendors in New York City declare war on the
trucking industry.

Merrill, Jean. The Superlative Horse. Viking, 1959.
Honor and duty are the guidelines of a peasant boy who
becomes head groom of an ancient Chinese stable.

Morey, Walt. Gentle Ben. Dutton, 1965.
The story of friendship between a boy and a bear.

Snyder, Zilpha. The Velvet Room. Atheneum, 1965.
The desire to escape from everyday life leads Robin to
a secret room.

Stevenson, William.   The Bushbabies.   Houghton, 1965.
A young girl and her native guide encounter danger in
the African bush country.

Tolkien, John.   The Hobbit: Or, There and Back Again.
Houghton, 1938.
A home-loving hobbit leaves home in search of gold,
and encounters adventures with many strange creatures.

Chapter 5

DEVELOPING SKILLS FOR INDEPENDENT STUDY

The Neglected Primary Grades

Students in kindergarten through grade three are often neglected when consideration is being given to the development of the work/study skills program in the school. The prevailing opinion in many elementary schools centers around the idea that the primary child's day is so filled with acquiring the basic skills of reading and mathematics that there is little time for the addition of other material to the primary curriculum. The point missed is that introducing primary research skills as early as the kindergarten years is not an addition to the curriculum but a functional application of those skills included in the curriculum.

The public library recognizes the need for introducing children to books quite early in life through sponsoring pre-school story hours and summer activities for pre-school and primary grade children. The school library frequently ignores the very young with the exception of an occasional story hour or selecting books for pleasure reading.

Simple research and reference skills can be acquired by primary students and should be introduced in a functional situation in the kindergarten program and developed throughout the elementary school years. The skills taught should be those that primary students will use and the teaching of any skill should be followed immediately by the application of the skill by the student.

The Scope and Sequence Chart which follows will indicate the range of skills that should be acquired by primary students by the end of the third grade.

Primary Skills: Scope and Sequence

Skill	Taught & Reinforced at Grade			
	K	1	2	3

Library Citizenship
Developing a proper attitude toward
the rights and property of others

	K	1	2	3
	X	X	X	X

To learn the care of books and other
library materials

	X	X	X	X

To develop purposeful study habits in
the classroom and the media center

	X	X	X	X

To stress the responsibility of the individual in a group situation

	X	X	X	X

Library Use
To acquire the view of the library as
a place containing many carriers of
knowledge

	X	X	X	X

To learn the varied uses of these carriers
of knowledge in practical situations

	X	X	X	X

To accept the librarian as one who is
willing and able to assist students with
questions and problems

	X	X	X	X

To learn the procedure for borrowing
and returning materials

	X	X	X	X

To learn the location of the types of
materials found in the library

			2	3
			X	X

Parts of a Book
To understand the terms title, author,
illustrator and publisher and to locate
these in a book

			2	3
			X	X

To understand the terms title page,
contents, glossary and index and to be
able to locate information in the book
through the use of the glossary, contents and index

			2	3
			X	X

To understand the meaning of the term

	K	1	2	3
Taught & Reinforced at Grade				
copyright date and the importance of this date to the research process				X
Locating Fiction				
To understand the meaning of the term, fiction			X	X
To know how books of fiction are shelved in the library			X	X
To know how records, tapes and film-strips of favorite stories are housed in the library			X	X
To be able to locate a book of fiction if given the last name of the author			X	X
To understand that all of an author's books of fiction will be found together in the library			X	X
Locating Nonfiction				
To be able to define the term, nonfiction			X	X
To know that nonfiction books are shelved in number order			X	X
To understand the call number as the address of the book in the library			X	X
To be able to locate a book of nonfiction if given the title or subject and the Dewey number			X	X
Reference Books				
To understand the meaning and use of a dictionary (primary) or pictionary	X	X	X	X
To be able to locate an entry in a primary dictionary	X	X	X	X
To understand the parts of a primary dictionary entry	X	X	X	X
To understand the function of a set of				

	Taught & Reinforced at Grade			
	K	1	2	3
primary encyclopedias		X	X	X
To be able to select the volume needed according to subject			X	X
To be able to locate an entry in the encyclopedia and to search for and find a specific answer to a question			X	X
To be able to prepare a simple research report and to present information to the class	X	X	X	X

Activities for Developing Skills in the Primary Grades

Citizenship Activities

1. The teacher or librarian should read the following story and encourage student participation when pauses are reached. Discussion of the story may follow.

Our Library Visit

Our class went to the library. While we were there we saw many boys and girls reading _____ and working on _____. Some boys and girls were busy finding answers to questions. So that we would not disturb the other boys and girls, the librarian asked us to come in ____. We heard a story and chose books to take home. We signed our names on the _____ and gave the _____ to the librarian. When we are good library citizens everyone enjoys the library visit.

2. Care of books and library materials. Students should be encouraged to discuss ways of caring for books. Transparencies showing the right and wrong way to care for materials can be displayed and students urged to give reasons why a method shown is correct or incorrect. This activity can be followed with poems or drawings on the care of library materials which can be displayed in the center.

3. The Story Hour. The primary story hour should

be related to units of work undertaken in the classroom to
help primary students to see that library materials can expand their knowledge about a subject.

4. <u>Library Use</u>. On initial library visits students
should be allowed to explore the resources of the library.
Pictures of books, filmstrips, records, tapes, projectors of
all kinds, record players, tape recorders and any other material that the media center contains can be cut out of old
catalogs and mounted on heavy cardboard backing. Each
child should receive several of these picture cards and be
allowed to explore the library, searching for material or
equipment pictured on the card. Finding the material on his
own will help the student to remember the resources the
center has to offer when a need for such resources arises.

5. During library visits primary students should be
encouraged to observe the activities undertaken by other
students working in the center, and to tell why these activities may be necessary.

6. <u>A Listening Activity</u>. Students should be asked to
listen to the story about library helpers. Five library helpers are mentioned in the story. Following the story, students should be asked to recall as many of the helpers as
they can.

Library Helpers

Many people make our library a pleasant place to
visit. The librarian knows more about the library
than anyone else. She can help us to find good
books to read or to find answers to our questions.
Sometimes she tells us stories or shows films.
She helps us to learn how to use the library.

The library aide checks out our books. She shows
us how to use the equipment in the library. When
we return our books we take them to the library
aide.

The student helpers put the books and other materials back where they belong. Sometimes student
helpers bring books to our room. If the librarian
is busy the student helpers or the library aide can
help us to find books.

The custodian works to keep the library neat and
clean.   If something is broken he can fix it.   When
new books are delivered to the school the custodian
brings them to the library.

I am a library helper too.   I help other boys and
girls by working quietly in the library.   I help the
library aide and student helpers by putting books
back where they belong if I decide that I don't want
them.   I help the custodian by picking up any
paper that I see and putting things away neatly.

Follow up the story by asking: Who helps us to find answers
to our questions?   Who checks out our books?   Who shelves
the books?   Who keeps the library clean?   Who helps all of
the library helpers?

7.   Understanding the Role of the Librarian.   Students
can be encouraged to state ways in which the librarian has
been of help to them or ways in which they have seen the
librarian help others.   These can be listed on the board for
class discussion.

8.   Borrowing books and other materials.   Each child
should be given a book card and allowed practice time in
completing the information required on the card after demonstration by the teacher or librarian.   This should be done
immediately preceding an activity when children will be borrowing materials.

Parts of a Book

9.   After writing and illustrating their own stories,
students should make a simple book with cover, title page,
table of contents, glossary and index.   The book might contain several stories.

10.   Guess what page I see?   One student can give a
page number from a basic text and ask other students to
name the part of the book on which that page is found (index,
title page, text, glossary, table of contents).

11.   A display of books by one or more favorite authors can be set up in the room.   Children might read the
books together and write to the author telling which book
they liked best.

12.   A favorite book can be recorded on tape with directions as to where to begin in the book to read along as the tape plays.

13.   Children might collect favorite stories from old magazines to bind into book form complete with a table of contents.

14.   Original book covers or jackets of favorite books can be made by students giving the title, author, publisher and illustrator.

15.   Throughout the year students can write short criticisms of books read, giving their reaction to the book. These can be bound into booklets and exchanged with other students to share reactions.   Similar criticisms can be written about records of filmstrips of favorite stories that children have heard or viewed.

Locating Fiction

16.   To introduce the concept that books of fiction are shelved alphabetically by the author's last name, borrow a number of books of fiction from the library for the reading table.   Have students place these in order as they would be shelved in the library.

17.   Send a committee to the library to select books for the class reading table.

18.   Let each student choose a favorite author. Allow students to visit the library individually or in small groups to find books by the author they have chosen.

19.   Allow a committee of students to select books of fiction for the class on a particular subject--pets, fairy tales, etc.

20.   Use individual students or small groups to locate and preview records or filmstrips of favorite stories and to choose those which will be used in a class presentation.

21.   Children can select five favorite books from the library and make a "Favorite Book" list to be posted in the room for others to see.   The list should be made alphabetically by the author's last name.

22.   Ask a child to name a favorite author and tell
whether his books would be found near the beginning, middle
or end of the fiction section.   The child who answers correctly can then name his favorite author.

23.   Book Reviews on Tape.   Have children write
book reviews to be read on tape.   At the end of each review
tell where the book is located in the library.   Other children
might listen to the tape to learn about stories they might
enjoy.

Locating Nonfiction

24.   Ask the librarian to give students a tour of the
nonfiction section.   During the tour she should point out that
the books are shelved in number order and that each book
has a number (or an address) to show where it belongs in
the library.

25.   Borrow a collection of nonfiction titles from the
library for the room reading table.   Ask a committee to put
the books in order by their number.

26.   From old magazines cut pictures of familiar objects (horse, dog, boat, train, flower, etc.), mount on
cardboard and write the Dewey number for the subject be-
neath the pictures.   Allow children individually or in small
groups to visit the library and bring back a nonfiction book
with the same number and subject as shown on the card.

27.   Hidden Book Reports.   Ask children to tell about
a favorite book while keeping the book hidden.   Students are
to tell whether the book is fiction or nonfiction.   The student
who first guesses correctly can give his hidden book report.

Reference Books

28.   Making a dictionary.   Select a subject related to
a unit of work and ask children to list as many names as
they can, related to the subject.   (Example: pets) Have students place the names in alphabetical order and write one
sentence describing the pet.

29.   A dictionary of places or people.   Follow the
above procedure, with names of places with which children
are familiar or with names of famous people.

30.   Make frequent use of picture dictionaries in the classroom to acquire the meanings and spelling of unfamiliar words or terms.

31.   Make a list of five to ten simple topics.   Allow small groups or individuals to visit the library to determine in which volume of the encyclopedia the topic might be found. When volume numbers are correct, the group can then locate the page on which the topic is located and write the page number beside the volume number.

32.   Using the research form which follows, allow individual students or small groups to visit the library to locate the answer to a question with the help of the librarian. The first sentence is completed before leaving the classroom. The remainder of the form is completed in the library and students bring back the reference that they used to show to the class.

WHAT I LEARNED IN THE LIBRARY

Dear Parents:

In our class we are learning about _____ _____.   Each of us had a question to answer. My question was _____
_____
_____

Our school library has books, magazines, records, tapes, pictures, and filmstrips to help me find answers to my questions.   To find the answer to this question I used _____

The answer to my question is:_____
_____
_____
_____

Here is a picture about what I have learned.

Developing Skills in the Intermediate Grades

Guidelines for Instruction

No matter what skill it is necessary for a student to acquire, certain basic guidelines must be uppermost in the mind of the teacher and librarian if the skill is to be successfully mastered. Foremost is the premise that the student must have a need for the skill and must be given opportunity to immediately apply the skill in a functional situation. This basic tenet for the successful acquisition of skills is often overlooked and is possibly the greatest reason for the lack of success of many skills programs.

Gathering an entire class together and presenting a talk or film on the parts of a book, or the Dewey Decimal System, or whatever, is an archaic practice which has little value in any modern learning program. It may be that large group instruction can at times be successful, but for the student who has no need for a particular piece of information, the information itself is useless and attempting to present it to an entire class is an exercise in futility. The successful road to the acquisition of work/study skills lies in the student's need for an application of the skill. This cannot be overemphasized.

A second premise that must be kept in mind before a program of skill development can be initiated is that the acquisition of any skill must involve the more important skills of critical thinking and independent judgment. Every step in the research process requires evaluation on the part of the student. To locate materials the student must evaluate and choose among sources. To acquire specific knowledge he must be able to distinguish the real from the fanciful, fact from opinion, and the significant from the less significant. He must evaluate the information gained in light of his own experience and draw conclusions based on his evaluation. In organizing and recording information he must develop a logical sequence of data or events and determine cause and effect as well as pertinent details. In preparing the presentation he must know the needs of the group to whom the presentation will be made and strive for a presentation that will keep the interest of the group. This functional approach which stresses independent judgment should be well established by the beginning of grade four, and expanded throughout the elementary years. Assuming that students have gone through the primary skills program, the following chart indicates those skills which should be stressed in grades four through six.

Work/Study Skills

Scope and Sequence Chart
Grades 4-6

Locational Skills

Understanding and use of alphabetical order by first, second, third and fourth letter

Understanding and use of the call number for fiction

Ability to locate nonbook materials by call number

Understanding of the Dewey Number as a symbol of location and subject identification

Ability to locate library materials by the Dewey Number

Understanding of and ability to use an index

Understanding of the information contained on a catalog card

Ability to differentiate between title, author and subject cards

Understanding and use of the card catalog as an index to all materials contained in the media center

Understanding of the nature, purpose and use of basic reference tools, including:
    General Encyclopedia
    Science Encyclopedia
    History Encyclopedia
    Standard Dictionary
    Geographical Dictionary
    Biographical Dictionary
    Thesaurus
    Atlas
    Almanac
    Readers' Guide

Skills of Acquisition

Understanding of the purpose for reading or the purpose of the research activity

Ability to grasp main ideas

Ability to locate details related to the main idea

Skimming skills

Understanding of major topics and sub-topics in an article

Ability to follow sequence of ideas or events

Ability to determine cause and effect

Ability to differentiate fact from opinion

Ability to differentiate the significant from the less significant

Ability to differentiate the real from the fanciful

Ability to develop and/or follow directions

Ability to summarize research material

Skills of Organization and Recording

Understanding of a bibliography and the ability to prepare a bibliography

Ability to take notes relevant to information required

Spelling skills

Ability to place facts in sequence

Ability to outline

Use of interesting words

Knowledge of grammar and sentence construction

Ability to write a well-organized report

Ability to evaluate the finished product

Skills of oral presentation

Organized and sequential

Clear speech

Able to present main points and details in order

Able to answer questions on the subject

Able to defend a stated position with relevant information

Activities for Developing Skills
in the Intermediate Grades

Locational Skills

1. Have groups of students file catalog cards above the rods in alphabetical order in the card catalog. Another group of students can check the placement of cards, referring to a simplified list of filing rules compiled by the librarian. Cards will be finally filed after a completed check by the librarian.

2. Each student is given three sample catalog cards. Students are to underline information on the cards as it is given by the teacher or librarian. Finally students are to find two of the three books indicated by the cards.

3. Definition game. One student gives a library term (call number, catalog card, etc.); the student who can first define the term then gives a term for others to define.

4. Have each student write on a paper the name of a famous person or place. Students exchange papers and using the card catalog list as many references as they can find about the person or place.

5. Develop a list of sample questions. Ask which type of catalog card would you seek to answer the question. Examples:

      A. Does the library have books by Laura Ingalls Wilder? (author card)

      B. Where can I read about the Gateway Arch? (subject)

C. Who was Charlotte Forten? (subject)

D. Does the library have a copy of Henry and Ribsy? (title)

E. Who illustrated The Biggest Bear? (title)

6. Selecting the key word. Each student develops a question of interest to him. He reads the question to the class asking class members to decide upon the key word in the question. The key word is to be used to check the reference in an index or the card catalog.

7. On 3 x 5 cards list one piece of information about a book--the title, author or subject. Students are to use the card catalog to locate the missing information and fill in the card.

8. Have students bring some favorite nonfiction books from home (these can include paperbacks). Students can decide as a group (after discussion) the general subject category in which the book would belong. A committee can check the subject in the card catalog to see if the class was correct.

9. Have students construct a table of contents, index and bibliography for a completed research report. A cover can be designed giving the title and author of the report and the report can be simply bound in book form.

10. Choosing the Right Index. List on a mimeographed sheet the major indexes found in your school library. These might include:

> Subject Index to Books for Intermediate Grades by Mary Eakin
>
> Abridged Reader's Guide to Periodical Literature, H. W. Wilson Co.
>
> National Geographic Magazine Cumulative Index, 1947-1963
>
> Index to Fairy Tales, Myths and Legends by Mary Eastman
>
> Index to Children's Poetry by John E. Brewton

Index to the New Book of Knowledge, Grolier

Ask students to search in the library for the index which will contain the following references and list those books where the article, poem or story will be found:

Gorgon's Head, the Story of Perseus

An article on Africa in 1950

Poems of Robert Louis Stevenson

A magazine article on drugs

Christmas stories for older boys and girls

Information on the United States Army

11. Guide word quiz. Each student can develop a guide word quiz based on the use of guide words in the dictionary. Questions can be exchanged with other students and the dictionary checked for the answer if the student is not sure. A sample question might be: (True or false: The word "branch" would appear on a dictionary page with the guide words "brain" and "brave").

12. Word tree. A word is placed on the branch of a tree mounted on the bulletin board. Using the Thesaurus or dictionary of synonyms, students find other words with the same meaning. The tree should be covered with word leaves by the end of the day. New words can be chosen each day.

13. Which encyclopedia is best? Students should be allowed browsing time with the various types of encyclopedias located in the media center. Each student should be provided with a list of questions and should indicate after each question which encyclopedia would be the best to consult for the answer. Sample questions might be:

What route did Paul Revere follow on his famous ride? (History)

What is the origin of Mother's Day? (General)

In what way are icebergs a danger to man? (Science)

Students can then select one question of interest to them and locate the answer to report to the class.

14.   Selecting one article in an encyclopedia, list the major topics and the sub-topics in the article.   Develop questions based on the article and ask students under which major topic or sub-topic they would look to locate the answer. Students may check their answers by using the encyclopedia and looking under the topic they selected for the answer to the question.

15.   Select one map in the Atlas for study.   Develop questions which may be answered by studying the map.   Example: Map of Australia.

Which state on the map is largest in territory?

Give the location symbol for the capital of Western Australia.

What similarity do you notice about all capitals?

16.   Finding key words in questions.   List questions that contain more than one topic on 3 x 5 cards.   Have students underline the major topic with one line and the sub-topic with two lines in each question.   Students may then check the index to the almanac and locate the answer which may be written on the card.   Examples:

Starley invented the modern bicycle in what year?

When was the San Francisco earthquake?

How many air miles is it between New York City and St. Louis, Mo. ?

17.   The Geographical Dictionary--differentiating entries.   List place names that are similar in some way.   Ask students to differentiate between them.   Example: Tell whether the Fort listed is a town or a military installation.

a)   Fort Fisher   d)   Fort LeBoeuf
b)   Fort Madison   e)   Fort Garry
c)   Fort Nelson   f)   Fort Lauderdale

18.   The Biographical Dictionary--interpreting an entry.   Select a common last name (Example: Smith).   Ask

students to use skimming skills to answer specific questions.
Example:

> Which two Smiths were of the same religious faith?
>
> Which Smith was teaching at the University of
> Chicago until the time of his death?
>
> What was another occupation of the Smith who
> served as Secretary of State of Texas in 1845?

19. Allow students browsing time in the periodical
section of the library. Help them to become acquainted with
the many types of periodicals by having home copies brought
into the classroom. Ask students to list current topics of
special interest. Examples: Drugs, the Vietnam War, Ex-
trasensory Perception, etc. Allow each student to select
one topic from the list of interest to him. Using one or
more issues of the Abridged Reader's Guide, find articles
on the topic. Locate the periodical in which the article
appears and summarize the article for the class.

20. Reference Quiz. Ask each student to develop
one question of interest to the class. As each question is
read, students are to decide which reference book would be
the best to use to locate the answer. Differences of opinion
may arise and students should be encouraged to justify their
answers.

Skills of Acquisition

21. Reading or listening for main ideas. Students
read or listen to a story or an article. Main ideas are then
summarized. Details can then be listed concerning the subject and finally the reasons for the actions in the story or
the events determined.

22. Locating main ideas or topics in news articles.
When newspaper articles are analyzed for main ideas it will
be quickly discovered that the first paragraph of the article
contains the main idea, with less important details following.
After locating the main idea in the first paragraph, students
should note how many other details are included in the paragraph. Which detail is least important? (The last one
given.)

23. Determining fact from opinion. Ask students to

analyze the following statement (and other similar statements): Pigs are dirty animals. Use the following questions
to analyze the statement:

> What authority says this?

> What proof exists for the statement?

> Have I had any .experience to prove this to be true
> or untrue?

24. Telling the real from the fanciful. Place the
following statement on the board: The dragon's name was
Custard. Have students analyze the statement using the
following questions:

> Is this a real dragon or an imaginary one? Why?

> Do dragons really exist?

> How can I determine if dragons exist?

> Is this book fiction or nonfiction? Why?

25. Determining the recency of material. Place the
following statement on the board: Someday men may travel
to the moon. Students should analyze the statement using the
following questions:

> Would this book have a recent copyright date?
> Why or why not?

> In light of our current knowledge how accurate will
> the other information in this book be?

Skills of Organization and Recording

26. Notetaking. Ask students to fold a paper into
four parts. On the board or using a transparency, display
a sample note card. At the top of the card write the question to be answered. (Students develop four questions, one
for each note card.) Next write the word, "Source. " Students fill in the source they expect to use to find the answer.
Finally write the word. "Answer. " Students use media
center materials to locate the answer. The answer is written on the card. If a different source is used than the one
originally listed, a new note card should be made.

27. Have students exchange note cards, placing the
cards in order so that events are recounted in the sequence
in which they occurred. Note cards are then returned to the
owner who will check them to see if he agrees with the
order or wishes to make further changes. The four note
cards should then be developed into a simple outline with the
answer to each question becoming a sub-topic under the major topic.

28. If students require practice in outlining, a
familiar story can be outlined by the class, determining main
events in the story which will become main topics and lesser
events which will be details or sub-topics. Several stories
might be done in this way.

29. Individual students or a committee of students
can preview recordings or filmstrips and select those for
class presentation which best fit the topic at hand. The
committee should develop questions for the class to keep in
mind during the listening or viewing activity.

30. Books of historical fiction are good springboards
to creative writing combined with research. If some members of the class have together read such a book or heard a
recording, discussion might be centered around the type of
research the author had to do to write a believable story.
Students should be encouraged to research a period of history
of interest to them and use the facts gained to develop an
original story.

The Independent Study Activity

While it is highly desirable to give students the freedom to learn, it is usually wise to structure initial independent study activities until the teacher can be sure that
students have the necessary skills to complete them successfully. When the teacher and the librarian work closely with
the student, giving assistance only when it is needed, the
student will soon gain confidence to work more competently
alone. The teacher should inform the librarian of the type
of research project being undertaken by class members, and
of those students who may need more help than others.

If the initial activity is structured through the use of
a teacher-made outline, students may research the major
topics on the outline in any order, but the final presentation

should be placed in the order of the original outline. When
the outline is no longer needed, the following guide for independent study activities may prove useful:

Planning for Independent Study Activities in the IMC

Independent study activities in the elementary school
can be successful if careful planning precedes the activity.
Elementary media personnel, working cooperatively with the
classroom teacher, give careful supervision to students working in the center and assist in the development of those
skills essential to successful independent study.

Steps in Independent Study Activities

1.   The teacher sets the goals and objectives with
students to be achieved during a particular unit of work.

2.   Teacher-librarian planning conference. The
teacher gives the librarian the concepts to be developed during the unit, topics and sub-topics to be explored, and in-
forms the librarian of students with special learning difficulties.   Arrangements are made for the class as a whole
to visit the center and meet with the librarian, who will introduce materials to be used during the unit and stimulate
interest in their use.   If particular work/study skills need
to be taught or reinforced for use during the unit, skills
classes for groups or individuals will also be arranged.

3.   Students in the classroom survey the unit as a
whole and select a topic of interest to research.   Responsibility for research and reporting on topics can be assigned
individually or in committees depending on the needs of students and the type of material to be covered.

4.   Before visiting the IMC and after the topic has
been selected, students "brainstorm" both individually and in
small groups to determine what is to be learned about the
topic.   Questions to be answered are listed.   This step is
important in directing the student's thinking in a specific
direction and prevents the copying of large blocks of material from the encyclopedia or other reference.

5.   Following the listing of questions, the student
lists those sources of information most likely to have the

answers for him.   These sources include every main topic
or idea that might be found in the card catalog or indexes.
(For example: A student reporting on Samuel Mudd would
list as main topics to seek in an index or card catalog:
Mudd; doctor; physician; Lincoln, Abraham; Civil War; Booth,
John Wilkes; etc.) This is the real "think" phase of the independent study activity and prevents aimless wandering and
discouragement when the student reaches the IMC.

    6.   After topic, questions and sources are listed, the
student begins his search for information in the media center.   Media personnel are always ready to assist when difficulty arises in the search for information.   Skills for successful location of materials that have been taught are
actually learned in this phase of the project.

    7.   Taking notes.   When specific answers are found,
notes are taken on separate note cards listing the information
and its source.   This will require one or more periods of
classroom instruction before students are ready to take notes
on their own.

    8.   Outlining.   Notes are placed in outline form.
This might be the formal outline or an informal placing of
main points in correct sequence.

    9.   Writing the report.   The finished product should
be as correct as the student can make it.   This is the time
for self-evaluation, when students work toward a well-done,
finished product.   Now is the time for the teacher to empha-
size grammar, punctuation, capitalization, etc.

    10.   Presenting the report.   Students should be given
ample time to prepare their presentation.   They should be
encouraged to present the material in an interesting manner
of their own choosing: demonstrations, dramatizations, using
tapes, visuals, pictures, puppets, debates, quizzes or whatever method will best serve the student's purpose.

Pitfalls in the Independent Study Process

    In any successful independent study activity certain
difficulties must be overcome.   Among the major problems
which may arise are the following:

    A.   The student who chooses an activity to please

the teacher rather than selecting a topic of genuine interest
to himself.

B. Difficulty in selecting a topic. Many types of
motivational media are desirable for use when introducing a
new unit of work. The alert teacher will watch for sparks
of interest on the part of reluctant students when media are
used for motivational purposes.

C. Students who have learned the system. The so-
called bright students are usually those who have achieved
success in school through the ability to work through a highly
structured situation, doing well on the answer sheet or workbook page. These students tend to rebel when placed in the
somewhat unstructured independent study situation, and need
special guidance to feel comfortable in the new situation.

D. Lack of understanding of the topic to be researched. A student who does not know what he is seeking
will have little success in finding it.

E. Spelling. In order to use an index or the card
catalog, correct spelling is essential. Main topics should
be written and spelled correctly before the search for information begins.

F. The tendency on the part of the teacher to move
the entire class along the same path at the same time.
Students do not proceed through all steps at the same time.
The teacher must be sure that the student is ready for each
step before he proceeds to that step. A student who has
mastered the skills needed for each phase of the independent
study activity is not likely to become discouraged.

G. The need to check progress. The student's
progress must be checked often to be sure that he understands and is following through with the activity at hand.
While some students are working in the media center, other
students are receiving help in the classroom. Careful planning is required on the part of the teacher to assure the
progress of each student.

The form which follows can be used by students before beginning their search for information, to clarify their
thinking about not only the information to be located but the
best reference sources to be used. The initial use of the
form will help the student to achieve success in his first

Name _____

Research Report

TOPIC:_____

QUESTIONS THAT I WANT TO HAVE ANSWERED ABOUT
THIS TOPIC

1. _____
2. _____
3. _____
4. _____
5. _____
6. _____
7. _____
8. _____

SOURCES OF INFORMATION

A. Card catalog: Topic(s)_____
   _____

B. Encyclopedia: Topic(s)_____
C. Geographical Dictionary: Topic(s)_____
D. Famous First Facts: Topic(s)_____
E. Atlas: Topic(s)___·_____
F. Almanac: Topic(s)_____
G. Periodicals: Title(s)_____
H. Indexes: Topic(s)_____
I. Biographical Dictionary_____
J. Other:

independent study activity.   When students become adept at
the procedure the form may no longer be needed.

Chapter 6

NONBOOK MATERIALS IN THE RESEARCH PROCESS

A Look at Individual Differences

If one were to question almost any classroom teacher concerning likeness among his twenty-five to thirty students, he would readily admit that few existed. Physical differences would most likely be pointed out, followed quickly by a resumé of the differences in background, interests, and learning ability, as well as the varied levels of achievement found in any classroom. The teacher might also state that he attempts to individualize instruction by placing materials in the hands of students that they are able to handle easily. However, closer questioning would probably reveal that the "materials" used for individual instruction are basic textbooks assigned to students on the basis of a readability level achieved on a standardized test of some type. In other words, regardless of the wide span of individual differences found among students in any classroom, every student is expected to learn in the same way--through the reading of a basic text.

As noted earlier, before he enters school the child has been exposed to and has learned from a variety of audiovisual experiences including television, radio, the phonograph, the tape recorder, photographs, motion pictures, billboards, signs, the telephone, travel and advertisements, as well as human association. From these experiences the child has learned. to think, to speak, to act and react, to develop values, to integrate knowledge, to form opinions, and to develop concepts. Yet the school often labels the child who has difficulty in learning to read as one who is "slow to learn!" Perhaps it is easier to question the child's ability to learn than to question the methods we use to teach.

Most basic teaching today follows the development of a concept from a series of small steps or ideas that must be gained one at a time until a final concept or idea is reached. Yet, when the child leaves the classroom and turns on the

117

television at home, he is exposed to some very complex
processes or ideas which he appears to grasp instantly without all of the prerequisite groundwork that is considered so
necessary in the classroom. Most twelve-year-olds can give
a fairly accurate explanation of what occurs in an atomic ex-
plosion, or a description of weightlessness in space, or the
effects of the use of marijuana versus the use of heroin--all
ideas or concepts gained without benefit of reading a basic
text, or through developing a line of thought step-by-step
until a conclusion was reached. Through audio-visual means,
today's student is continually exposed to the learning process
both before and after school hours, but the process sometimes comes to a halt during the school day when the teacher
deprives the student of the type of learning experience from
which he has achieved his information most comfortably and
substitutes, instead, the basic text.

Prerequisites for Learning

        For positive learning to take place the student must
be intrinsically motivated toward the learning situation; he
must be interested in the subject; he must feel comfortable
with the learning vehicle; and he must be able to relate the
material to be learned to his own experience. If these
factors are not in evidence the child will soon develop negative feelings about the whole business of formal education
and refuse to accept any learning experience that is connect-
ed with the school. It cannot be overemphasized that how a
child feels about the learning situation is far more important
than the actual subject matter to be learned, for only when
a child feels comfortable and successful in a learning activity
will he achieve specific educational goals.

The Role of Multi-Media

        Through the use of multi-media experiences the
teacher can appeal to more than one of the senses of his
students. A filmstrip or recording may provide motivation
and interest that cannot be achieved through the use of the
text alone. A student may feel comfortable reading captions
on a filmstrip and uncomfortable attempting to gain the same
information from a book. Other students may readily accept
a book in the form of microfiche since this means of viewing relates directly to the television experience with which
they are familiar. These students might not accept the same

book in its hard-cover form.   A student with difficulty in
hand/eye coordination may welcome the opportunity to present a report orally through the use of the tape recorder,
rather than losing interest in the subject during his struggle
for neatness and legibility in a written report.

     The role that multi-media can play in the learning
experience is many-faceted.   Through the use of audio-visual
experiences the teacher can help each child find and use that
material with which he will most likely succeed, and build
upon those successes to develop skills considered necessary
in our literate world.

     It is the responsibility of the classroom teacher to
use audio-visual materials effectively.   Just as the teacher
attempts to provide written material on a readability level
suitable for the individual student, the teacher must also be
aware not only of the content but the level of comprehension
required for the use of any audio-visual software.   To use a
filmstrip with an entire class group is just as poor a teaching technique as placing the same book in the hands of every
student and expecting all children to get the same level of
information from it.   The major value in the use of audio-
visual materials lies in individualization of instruction.   The
medium selected for a learning experience with an individual
or small group of students depends on the concept to be developed, the background knowledge of the students, the level
of understanding of the students, and the enthusiasm of students (or lack of same) for the use of the medium.   The use
of media is not a substitute for good teaching but an invaluable aid to it.

Selection of Audio-Visual Materials

     The major responsibility for the selection of audio-
visual materials lies with the media specialist or librarian
in the school.   In working closely with the classroom teacher
and students, the librarian, more than any other person in
the school, should be aware of the demands for materials
being made on the media center.   In meeting those demands
the following questions must be resolved before new material
is purchased or older material discarded:

     1.   Is the material suitable for the age and grade level
          for which it is intended?

2. Does the material meet the specific demands of the curriculum for which it was requested?

3. How recent is the material? Is recency a factor in the selection of the material?

4. Will the method of presentation keep the interest of the listener or viewer?

5. What is the scope of the medium? Does it cover an entire subject or one facet of the subject?

6. Is the style suitable for the subject? (Example: Do we want a recording of the Jungle Book produced by Walt Disney Enterprises for entertainment, or a serious recording of this classic by Kipling for study?)

7. Is the format offered the best one in which to buy the material? (Example: Should we buy The True Book of Reptiles in filmstrip or microfiche form?)

8. Does the demand for a particular item justify the cost?

9. Is the technical quality of the production good, fair, or poor?

10. How does the material compare with other materials on the subject developed in similar format?

While media personnel must accept the responsibility for applying selection criteria when considering materials for purchase, the selection of materials should be a cooperative process; those who will use the media should be consulted and involved in the process. Faculty members should be informed of new materials available in their area, and these should be obtained for preview before purchase by those who will use them. Previewing of materials is a time-consuming but necessary activity, for the most expensive materials in any library are those that do not meet the needs of students and teachers and consequently take up valuable space without being used.

The Use of Audio-Visual Materials in the Research Process

      A number of basic concepts can be grasped more
easily through the use of nonprint materials than through employment of the printed page.   One of the most obvious of
these is sound.   A student whose major research purpose is
to be able to identify the calls of one or more species of
birds will find little help from a book.   However the use of
the recording, Songbirds of America (Houghton Mifflin
6-83829), will suit his purpose very well.   The stages of
plant growth have been recorded through time lapse photo-
graphy to lead the student to an instant understanding of these
stages within a space of a very short time.   Through the use
of the film loop the student can watch, as many times as
necessary, a spider spin its web, or the use of the potter's
wheel, or a demonstration of the dissection of a frog or
numerous other situations which cannot be brought to life on
the printed page.

      Concepts of size are more readily understood through
the use of the motion picture or television, as are concepts
of space, time and motion.   Careful selection and use of
nonbook materials serve to broaden and extend any research
activity.   Whether the final product of the activity is a map,
chart, bulletin board, student-produced film, report, tape
recording or transparency presentation, each step in the
preparation of the presentation requires the student to use
the basic skills of research.   He must be able to locate both
print and nonprint sources and evaluate them as to accuracy,
content, relevancy, and ultimate use.   He must determine
the authority for the material, separate fact from opinion
and the significant from the less significant, and be able to
integrate the new knowledge with knowledge he already pos-
sesses.   In evaluating the information gained in the light of
his own knowledge and experience he must draw conclusions
and present those conclusions in a clear and efficient manner.
The activities which follow are designed to provide this type
of learning experience.

Bulletin Boards

      Bulletin boards can be used to introduce a unit of
study, to stimulate curiosity in a concept or idea, to arouse
interest, to develop questions or to foster critical observa-
tion.   Student production of bulletin boards can provide an
invaluable learning experience.   Such construction involves

many research techniques.   The basic subject of the board
must be determined, defined and clarified.   Material must be
gathered which is relevant to the concept to be developed.
All material must be related to a single idea and should be
so organized that the idea is easily grasped by those viewing
the board.   Not only must the central theme be easily seen
but it must be presented with unity, balance and purpose.

Artistically, the bulletin board should be of good composition, eye-catching, colorful, in good taste and uncluttered.
The development of a good bulletin board will not only provide research activity for an individual or group of students
but will give students with artistic talent an opportunity to
combine that talent with research skills.

Charts, Graphs, Posters and Study Prints

The wide exposure of today's youth to advertising has
made many students experts in evaluating the still picture or
display designed to illustrate a single point or theme. Study
questions can be developed by the teacher or by students to
guide other students in the use of still pictures.   The use of
charts, posters, or other forms of graphic representations
can be a springboard to the development and research of
questions on the subject, or can be a culminating activity
demonstrating the concepts developed during a unit of work.

The advantages of using charts, graphs, posters or
study prints are several.   They represent in graphic form,
information that would take many pages of printed material
to explain.   When the printed experience is transformed into
a visual image, greater student participation in the explanation of the picture or the development of questions concerning
the still projection is possible.   The use of graphs can show
at a glance complex growth rates, or costs or production
methods, and provides the best means of comparing factors
under discussion.   The ability to combine data for presentation in graph form is an excellent indication of the level of
critical thinking developed by any student.

It is well to keep in mind that the use of still pictures, charts or graphs will achieve best results in small
group situations, for few charts or study prints are large
enough to be seen in detail by large groups.   Because the
picture or chart is a static medium it must be changed frequently for it will not retain interest over a long period of

time. Occasionally, storage of these materials is a problem
because of diversity of size.   However, still pictures do
have an important role to play in increasing class participation, discussion and development of questions for research on
a particular subject, and in fostering research methods and
critical thinking.

Films

The use of the 8mm or 16mm motion picture or the
film tape can provide for reinforcement and extension of previous knowledge through the viewing of a realistic experience.
The motion picture is a medium which most students accept
as an integral part of their lives, having had the film experience via television from an early age.   Because they are
comfortable with the medium they tend to accept the information that it carries.   The use of the motion picture can
introduce concepts of time, motion, size, space and sound
that can be acquired in only one other way--through actual
experience.   Abstractions can be understood through the use
of this vicarious experience that might never be possible
through the student's own personal experience.

There are, of course, disadvantages to the use of
film.   The tendency of students to suspend judgment while
viewing motion pictures must be considered and provided for.
Equipment is not always in usable condition, films do not always arrive when scheduled, and once started, the film is
usually run all the way through.   During the showing of the film,
student participation is at a minimum, action moves too
rapidly for questions and if rear screen projection is not
available, a darkened room usually prohibits the taking of
notes.   However, provision for these difficulties can be made
in several ways.

1.   If available, several films on the same subject
can be previewed by a student group to select the most appropriate film for viewing by other groups.   The students
selected for this experience must have researched the topic
beforehand and must decide upon the concepts and details
that should best be presented by a film.   In viewing each
film a checklist of these concepts or details can be followed.
At the end of the viewing, checklists are compared through
discussion and a decision is made on the film to be selected.
It is then necessary for the group to develop the main points
in the film and present the points to those who will view it.

This same group of students can lead discussion on the major ideas of the film after the showing.

2. A film can be shown to a group twice: the first time with the sound, and the second without sound but with students providing the narration. This will provide an evaluation for the teacher of how well students were able to grasp the main ideas of the film.

3. Student film productions. Determining a subject, developing main ideas and deciding upon the best means to present those ideas are research skills involved in student production of 8mm films. In their own film productions, students must not only develop a working script that will enable them to present an idea without sound or use the tape recorder to accompany the film with sound; they must avoid bias and untrue statements in their presentation, be specific in approach and be able to present a concept in such a way that student viewers will grasp its meaning. These basic requirements pre-suppose a careful research process, a selection of relevant and meaningful data and a sequential organization of ideas.

4. Provision should be made for individual viewing of films related to the particular research process at hand. Once again, it is important that the student viewing the film be able to comprehend the major concepts presented. This requires on the part of the teacher or media specialist a knowledge of film content, the research needs of the student and the achievement level of the student.

Filmstrips

The filmstrip is one of the most widely used media forms in the elementary school. It is relatively inexpensive and may be presented as slowly or as rapidly as necessary. It is easy to use, does not require a completely darkened room and can be viewed by large groups, using the filmstrip projector, or by individuals, using the filmstrip viewer. While it is a means of still projection with motion only suggested, the filmstrip can show in graphic form people or events from other times, or places not generally available for direct viewing. Filmstrips can become outdated, and they should then be promptly discarded. They can also be damaged easily if not wound carefully and returned to their container correctly. An often overlooked bit of instruction

in how to avoid cinching will minimize the problem of damage. Students should be taught the care of nonbook materials just as they are taught to care for printed materials.

Research Activities with Filmstrips

1. The IMC should house a large collection of filmstrips for investigation. They should be cataloged and easily
accessible to students for individual viewing. In using filmstrips as a part of the data-gathering process, the student
will be required not only to locate information but to verify
facts from several sources before forming his conclusions,
compiling the data and organizing his discoveries into an
easily understandable presentation.

2. Many sound filmstrips are uncaptioned. Students
can view these filmstrips without sound or caption and research the data necessary to develop a script to accompany
the showing of the filmstrip to a group or class.

3. Creative Writing Activities. The use of uncaptioned story filmstrips can provide the stimulus for creative
writing activities. The filmstrip selected should be one with
which students are not familiar. Each child's attempt at
telling or writing a story should be accepted as the story he
sees. There is no right or wrong interpretation of the filmstrip in creative writing activities. It is simply an interpretation of a visual experience as the child relates it to his
own experience. When a filmstrip is used for this type of
activity, the sound portion should not be presented at any
time.

4. Simultaneous filmstrip/slide presentations. The
selection of slides and filmstrips to be shown at the same
time to broaden or present a concept requires the student to
integrate related experiences in order to develop a central
idea. Student production of slides using clear contact paper
and clay-based photographs or drawings from magazines is
a relatively simple and inexpensive process.

5. Student-produced slide presentations. In selecting materials pertinent to a problem and developing a sequential slide presentation, the student will employ all of the
basic research skills. His problem must be carefully defined; the material selected to present the problem must
graphically portray a main idea or theme. The student must

not only have a clear understanding of the concept to be presented but should know the group to whom the presentation is to be made and strive for a presentation that will be of interest to the group.

The Cassette Recorder

While earlier reel-to-reel tape recorders were often heavy, cumbersome, expensive and somewhat difficult to operate, the cassette recorder has largely eliminated these disadvantages. It is a very versatile piece of equipment, inexpensive, easy to operate and transport, and usable again and again. The storage of cassette tapes takes far less space than disc recordings and the cassette tape is not as easily damaged. In using the tape, the slow learner can listen again and again and take notes or illustrate a point while listening. The use of earphones for the listening experience keeps the attention of the learner on the material at hand. Sources of cassette tape material are numerous.

The cassette recorder, while not nearly as sophisticated as much of the hardware on the market today, can serve as a valuable tool in the discovery process. Each of the following action models employs as a constant the recorder, utilized in independent study programs to develop critical thinking. The recorder is one of the most important forms of media to use in the research process, i. e., in aiding students to develop the skills of location, acquisition, organization and recording.

Skills of Location and Acquisition

1. Basic Skill Tapes: The IMC should house a collection of locally or commercially produced tapes for developing the basic skills necessary to the independent pursuit of knowledge. Students who need instruction in a basic skill should have free access to the tapes and be able to listen with guidance from the media specialist until a particular process is understood. The listening activity should be undertaken only when the student has a need for it and should be followed by application on the part of the student of the skill presented.

2. The Talking Card Catalog: Tapes centering around frequently researched topics can be produced by

students reviewing the resources available in the media center on a particular topic. In student production of tapes critical thinking is essential for this is a means of integrating information rather than simply acquiring facts. The major value of each resource reviewed should be stated so that students using the tapes to locate material will not be misled concerning the basic point of view or content of the material.

3. An Encyclopedia on Tape: The IMC should house a large collection of tapes on a variety of topics. Many of these tapes can be locally produced and represent student research on a particular topic. Students making such a tape will be required not only to locate information, but to verify facts from several sources before forming conclusions, compiling the data, and organizing discoveries into an easily understandable presentation. Other students would approach the use of these tapes in the same manner as any research tool, i. e. , selecting data from the tape most relevant to the research process at hand.

4. Books that Speak: Students searching for books, either for information or for pleasure, should have access to a tape collection of "Books that Speak. " This collection would contain lively reviews of books on a variety of topics, for example, "Distant Lands, " "The World of the Supernatural, " "Famous People, " etc. When students record reviews of books about which they are truly enthusiastic, or hear interesting and enthusiastic reviews, they are more likely to become "turned on" to reading than through consulting an annotation on a catalog card.

5. Human Resources: Planning and recording interviews can be a valuable research activity for the interviewer and a source of primary research material for other students. Taped interviews with leaders in the community, business, industry, the fine arts, etc. will enlarge the school as a learning laboratory by making the community an integral part of the learning process.

Skills of Organization and Recording

6. Notetaking on Tape: Research data in the form of interviews or basic information can be recorded more easily on tape than on notecards. Notetaking on tape is especially valuable in group research activities where several

students are researching different aspects of a problem.
When taped notes are completed the group can listen to the
tapes together, selecting pertinent information and eliminat-
ing duplication of material. At this time the main points of
the group presentation can be noted and outlined.

        7. Recording the Presentation: The tape presenta-
tion, whether done by a group or individual, should have
four basic considerations: 1) a careful sequence of events
or ideas, 2) the inclusion of pertinent details, 3) a clear
presentation of cause and effect, and 4) the addition of
specific and clear directions, if necessary. In developing
this type of presentation students will indeed be required to
bring together ideas from many sources and to integrate
these ideas in a clear presentation of subject matter.

The Overhead Projector

        One of the major advantages in the use of the over-
head projector is that the teacher or student making the
presentation can face the class throughout the discussion of
material. Transparencies used on the overhead can be in
color or black and white, and overlays can be used to develop an idea in sequential steps if this is called for. The
projector is lightweight and can be transported easily, and
the occurrence of mechanical failure is minimal.

        When the overhead is used in a presentation, the
attention of the group can be focused on the projected image
or on the speaker simply by turning off the projector. In
addition to transparencies (which can be marked and written
upon while on the projector), objects with clear outlines or
shadow pictures can be projected.

        The initial cost of the projector is high, as is the
cost of most commercial transparencies. However, transparencies can be made from any drawing that a student
wishes to present, and if it is possible to obtain and wash
discarded X-ray film, this film can be used for producing
images, using a grease pencil either before or at the time
of the presentation.

        Major uses of the overhead projector are for the in-
troduction of material that may be new to the class, the
demonstration of a concept or technique, the explanation of
a process, reviewing materials which have been studied,

creative story telling, combined tape/transparency presentations, or for testing activities.

In preparing visuals for the overhead projector the student must first determine the idea or concept he wishes to present. Each visual should contain only one idea unless overlays are used to expand the concept. Using pencil, pen or felt marker, the student prepares the drawing for the visual on plain white paper. The drawing should be simple and uncluttered and any lettering should be large enough to be read easily when projected. Lettering should be kept to a minimum. Transparency film is then placed over the drawing and placed in a copier to make the visual.

The student presenting the visual should have a clear idea of the material to be presented and should prepare his oral presentation as carefully as he prepares the visual.

Creative Use of Visuals. Original short stories or poems can be illustrated and presented on visuals. This method of presentation allows the student to share his creative writing activity with others. A file of these original stories or poems can be kept in the materials center for use by teachers or students in storytelling activities. This type of activity is especially valuable in building collections of holiday material, for which there is a heavy, concentrated demand several times a year.

One major advantage of using the overhead projector for either research activities or creative writing is that presentations can be prepared far in advance and can be filed for use whenever needed.

Microforms

Microform has long been accepted as a research tool in the secondary school but has been slow to gain acceptance in the elementary school. With the introduction of inexpensive microfiche readers and the availability of books as well as periodicals for the elementary school on microfiche, this relatively inexpensive method of storing and retrieving information is now coming into wider use in the elementary field.

Many filmstrip titles, which cost between six and eight dollars, are now available in microfiche at one-half to one-sixth of the cost of filmstrips. When a number of

students are researching the same topic it is not unusual to
have several of them waiting to use the same filmstrip when
all projectors and viewers are in operation. The size of
the screen on the new microfiche projectors is large enough
to accommodate four to six students at one time. Viewing
material on microfiche together can promote group discussion of important points, of the relevancy and authority of
the material, and of the ultimate use of the material in the
research project.

        There are, of course, many different microforms
and they are not interchangeable within a single reader.
When and if a standardization of forms and equipment is
achieved, the task of selecting the best type of microform
and equipment will be easier.   However, the small amount
of storage space required for microform materials, combined with ease of information retrieval and use, should encourage media personnel to add microforms to the elementary materials center collection.

Records and Record Players

        Most students and teachers will readily accept records
as an integral part of the school program.   Recordings con-
stitute one medium with which most users are familiar and
therefore comfortable.   The tremendous variety of material
available on recordings and the ease of use of the record
player have made this one of the most popular types of
media in use in the elementary school today.

        Because recordings appeal to the audio sense only,
they provide an excellent vehicle for fostering listening activities and developing listening skills.   Used in a listening
center for small group or individual listening activities, recordings can bring to life historical events, scientific concepts, or the excitement to be found in a good story.

        The use of recordings can provide a valuable means
of developing reading skills in both the primary and middle
grades.   Students who have not developed a skill level high
enough to handle a particular book, in following a recording
of the book may develop skills of comprehension and word
recognition they are unable to attain through the printed page
alone.

        A number of recordings have been made of excellent

children's books and can be used with students to introduce
a particular book or to stimulate the desire to read a book
that may otherwise remain unnoticed. These recordings may
consist of a simple reading of a book or story, usually con-
densed to fulfill the time requirements of the recording, or
a dramatization of a book centering around the highlights of
the story. This type of record should be previewed to determine whether or not the spirit or style of the book has
been altered in fulfilling recording requirements. A poorly
done recording which does not carry the true impact of the
original printed form should not be used with students.

        A challenging research project for students is the
preparation of transparencies to accompany a recording. As
an example, during a transportation unit, a group of students
might listen to a recording about the lives and accomplishments of the Wright brothers. The listening experience is
followed by discussion of such questions as, "How were
people dressed in 1903?" "Where is Kitty Hawk?" "What
did this first airplane look like?" "What aerodynamic principles were involved in the construction of the plane?" Each
member of the group can then accept responsibility for researching and preparing a visual on one of the questions.
The recording can then be played for the class, accompanied
by student visuals and followed by student-directed class
discussion.

Television

        A number of studies have indicated that students
taught through the use of television learn as much as those
taught in conventional classrooms. Television presents an
opportunity to use many sources of audio-visual materials to
provide richer learning experiences. The television teacher
is usually a master teacher and it is possible for him to
bring to students material which may be too recent for inclusion in current textbooks. Students bring to the television
experience listening and viewing skills acquired from an
early and prolonged exposure to the medium.

        Because most educational television presentations are
based chiefly on the lecture method, opportunity must be
provided in the classroom for questions and discussion of
the topic at hand. The questions developed from the presentation should lead students to individual investigation of
topics. Since most educational television stations provide

the classroom teacher with guides to the various programs, the teacher, conferring with media personnel, can prepare in advance for the activities and use of materials which will follow the television program. The use of educational television requires careful planning and follow-up on the part of the teacher to assure active student participation in the learning situation.

Programmed Instruction

The use of programmed learning provides a means of individualizing instruction in a carefully organized, highly structured situation. Instructional programs are usually designed to present one or more concepts or ideas through a logical step-by-step presentation through which the student proceeds at his own pace. Programmed instruction may take the form of a programmed text, or the program may be housed in a teaching machine which enables the student to record his responses by pressing a button and receive immediate feedback concerning their correctness.

Programmed instruction is one means of developing basic skills but it is not as effective as bringing together knowledge from many sources, selecting material pertinent to a problem and forming opinions or drawing conclusions based on research. The use of programmed instruction does allow for individual differences and, if used correctly, can reinforce learning in the basic skill areas while at the same time releasing the time of the teacher to work with groups or individuals in independent study situations.

Summary

1. The use of audio-visual materials in the research process can be valuable in providing for individual differences.

2. A concept can be developed either by working from the major idea and filling in details, or through following a successive series of steps until the concept is developed.

3. For positive learning to take place the student must be intrinsically motivated, feel comfortable with the

learning vehicle, and be able to relate the material learned
to his own experience.

4. Through the use of audio-visual experiences the
teacher can help each child to find and use that material with
which he will most likely succeed, and can build upon those
successes to develop skills considered necessary in our
literate world.

5. Selection criteria should be established and followed before purchasing any type of media.

6. Concepts of sound, size, space, time and motion
are more readily understood through the use of audio-visual
materials.

7. Types of audio-visual materials and equipment
that can be utilized in the research process are bulletin
boards, charts, graphs, posters, study prints, films, filmstrips, the tape recorder, overhead projectors, microforms,
records, television and programmed instruction.

Chapter 7

THE SCHOOL AND THE COMMUNITY

The Separation of School and Community

From the beginning of our country's history through
the early 1900's the school and the community it served were
closely integrated. Both cultural and social activity of the
eighteenth, nineteenth and early twentieth centuries centered
around the church and the school. The proximity of the
school to the home made it the gathering place for community activity and the chief source of education and knowledge for all citizens of the community.

With the advent of electronic technology and subsequent
advances in both transportation and communication the sphere
of culture and learning expanded. As Americans became mo-
bile they sought increasingly wider avenues of culture and
learning and developed diverse forms of entertainment which
were totally unrelated to educational institutions. Schools
rapidly lost their role as major community centers and in
the 1970's now found themselves in danger of losing their major educational role.

The Community as a Learning Laboratory

If today's schools are to be successful in educating the
young greater involvement with the community must be sought
and achieved. In a world where it is possible to see, via
satellite communication and other sophisticated communications media, an event taking place in any part of the world
(and indeed, in outer space) at the instant it occurs, students'
knowledge of the world in which they live is often greater
than their knowledge of their own community. The short quiz
which follows will reveal some interesting data concerning the
knowledge or lack of knowledge that students (and teachers)
have of the community in which they live:

134

Community Quiz

1. What is the name of the mayor of your town?_____

   _____

2. What type of city government do you have?
   (a) Mayor and Aldermen   (b) City Manager and
                                   Council

3. What is the name of your Alderman or Council
   member?

4. Do you have a city health department?_____

5. Do you have a city hospital?   If so, where is it
   located?_____

6. Is your fire department a volunteer department or
   part of a fire district?_____

7. What cultural activities are available in your city?

   _____
   _____
   _____

8. Name three major industries in your city and tell
   what each produces.

   _____
   _____
   _____

While this quiz is quite brief, it is sufficient to determine
just how aware students are of their community.   The
average number of correct responses made by students in
grades four through eight is two, indicating that the schools
have done an excellent job of isolating themselves from the
community they are supposed to serve.

   Most educators would agree that if learning is to be
effective it must be relevant to the learner.   Yet, the actual
community in which a student lives is not often considered
relevant to his education.   First graders spend a considerable amount of time learning about "community helpers"
from a textbook.   Using a controlled vocabulary, the text
leads these six-year-olds through the daily activities of the
milkman, mailman, doctor, nurse, fireman, and storekeeper,

with the more "advanced" texts including the teacher, the librarian and the barber (pictured performing a 1940 butch-
type haircut!).

By second or third grade, students have advanced to
reading maps which again show a mythical community complete with fire station and city hall. Many fourth grade
social studies curricula take children to other parts of the
world, relating man's occupations to his physical environment. The fifth grade social studies generally covers a
broad overview of United States history, and by sixth grade
students are either reading about ancient Greece and Rome,
or are learning about our American neighbors, Central and
South America and Canada. The irony is that by sixth
grade, students are frequently asked to compare the com-
munities and governments of these countries with their own,
although their own community as a learning laboratory has
never been fully explored.

Schools Without Walls

Many schools have begun to expand the learning experiences of students in a variety of ways. The single text
approach to teaching has given away to a multi-text approach.
The multi-text approach has been partially replaced by the
multi-media approach. The single classroom, which for so
many years was a self-contained unit of learning, has given
away to subject specialists and separate classrooms for these
subject specialties in music, art, physical education and
science. In the more progressive schools libraries have become learning laboratories or multi-media centers for the
independent investigation of problems of the student's own
choosing. Thus, the walls of the classroom have been extended to include the outer walls of the schools. But the
basic need of today's students is greater than these limited
facilities will provide. The need now is for schools without
walls, to allow the development of a true spirit of inquiry
and the acquisition of knowledge relevant to the student's life
as he lives it in our modern society.

The form of most educational institutions is based on
a lock-step structure of learning. From grade level to grade
level and from one textbook level to the next, students
progress in a timed, orderly fashion. The student who rebels against this lock-step form of order is considered a
slow learner, a discipline problem, or an emotionally dis-

turbed child. The lock-step form of order is considered
essential because of the large number of students and the
limited funds with which the schools must work. New approaches frequently do cost money, and new approaches to
learning result in unpredictable learning outcomes. It is
difficult, if not impossible, to justify to taxpayers the expenditure of funds for learning activities which may have
negative outcomes. Because our society is based on the idea
of success, the learning value of a negative result is overlooked. While these factors may partially explain the con-
tinuance of self-contained schools, the major reason for their
existence is that operating a self-contained school requires
less effort than expanding the walls of the school into the
community. Only progressive administrators, energetic
teachers and innovative media personnel can, through their
combined efforts, take positive steps toward bringing the
school and the community together.

Locating Educational Experiences in the Community

Before attempting to locate community resources that
will add depth and breadth to the curriculum it is essential
to determine specific goals and objectives for such a program. What kinds of experiences will have real meaning for
boys and girls? Why do we want them to have these experiences? What learning outcomes do we expect from the
integration of school and community resources? No attempt
will be made here to set arbitrary goals and objectives for
each community, for each learning institution will have its
own specific goals based on the desires of its patrons for
the education of the young. But once these goals have been
determined, community leaders in government, the arts,
business and industry must be located and contacted, and
specific arrangements made for the broadening of student
learning experiences.

A study of the school's curriculum will reveal the
initial community resources to be contacted. The chart below is based on the social studies curriculum of grades 1-6.
Subject area listings are followed by the type of community
resource which may be available:

SOCIAL STUDIES CURRICULUM
Grades One through Six

Subject Area   Community Resource

Community Helpers   City Government Offices
and   Sanitation Department
City Government   Fire Department
                                     Health Department
                                     Hospital
                                     Food Inspection Office
                                     Street Maintenance
                                     Rabies Control Office
                                     Animal Shelter
                                     Library
                                     Police Department
                                     City Council Meetings
                                     Mayor
                                     Alderman or Councilman
                                     Municipal Courts

How We Get Food,   Packing House
Clothing and   Cannery
Shelter   Frozen Foods Plant
                                     Farm
                                     Bakery
                                     Supermarket
                                     Shoe Factory
                                     Clothing Factory
                                     Department Store
                                     Architect
                                     Home Builder
                                     Large Construction Firm

Indians and   Museums
Pioneer Life   Historical Societies
                                     Local Citizens with Historic
American History   Collections
                                     Local Authors
                                     Newspaper Morgue
                                     Libraries

Transportation   Bus Station
and   Railroad Station
Communication   Local Trucking Firm
                                     Airport
                                     Newspaper

Subject Area	Community Resource

Transportation and Communication	Telephone Office
	Radio Station
	Television Station
	Computer Center
	Factories which Produce
	  Aircraft, Trucks,
	  Automobiles,
	  Communications Equipment

Other Lands	Consular Offices of Foreign
	  Countries
	Import/Export Houses
	Businesses Dealing in
	  Foreign Goods
	Restaurants Specializing in
	  Foreign Foods
	Local Citizens or Visitors
	  from Other Lands
	Citizens Who Have Traveled
	  in Other Lands

The five basic areas cited in this initial list are matched with forty-seven community resources which can be tapped to enrich the curriculum and bring it alive for students. With a little creative thought, the list of resources available in the immediate or a nearby community can be endless.

When approached in a professional manner, community leaders are usually more than willing to make their facilities available for educational purposes. Many industries and businesses have in the past taken the initiative in this area by making their facilities available to student groups through scheduled tours or by supplying the schools with literature.

The initial contact with any business or industry should be by letter. The letter should clearly state the subject which students will be studying, the benefits that might accrue from such a class visit, the average age and the number of students. A form might be sent with the letter in duplicate to be completed by the personnel of the business or industry (with the duplicate to be kept by them).

Form for Contacting Community Resources

1. Name of the agency, business or company

    _____

2. Address

    _____

3. Major product or service of the agency, business
    or company

    _____

4. A brief description of what students might be ex-
    pected to see on the visit

    _____

    _____

    _____

5. Name of company personnel or office to be con-
    tacted to arrange for a visit

    _____

    Phone_____

6. Is the number of students who may visit limited?
    If so, please note maximum and minimum numbers.

    Maximum_____   Minimum_____

7. Is the age limit of students a factor to be consid-
    ered?

    _____ Minimum age of student visitors_____

8. Are specific times set aside for visitors?_____
    Time_____   Day(s)_____

9. Should visitors be requested to bring any specific
    item with them?

    _____

10. Is the type of wearing apparel of the visitors im-
    portant? If so, please describe.

    _____

11. How far in advance should the visit be arranged?

    _____

12. If there is a charge for the visit, please note
     below.

_____

Setting Up a Community Resource File

When forms have been received from the companies
contacted, a community resource file should be established
in the media center and made easily accessible to teachers
and students. This file can be on 3 x 5 cards and one person should be responsible for contacting community resources
and for maintaining and updating the file. Two cards are
suggested for the file, a main entry card using the company
or agency name as the heading and a subject card. The
sample card below will provide the needed information and
on the reverse side of the card notations can be made on
contacts and visits.

Waterford Meat Processing Company
1260 Winfield St.   New Haven
Phone: 838-7205

Visits: 9-5 M-F   Ages: 10 & up

Contact: Mr. Jacobs 838-7205
           2 weeks before
           Groups limited to 25
           Wear low-heeled shoes

NO CHARGE

MEAT PROCESSING: SLAUGHTERING,
                  CURING AND
                  SMOKING

If information concerning the visit is extensive, multiple cards can be used.

Following the visit, media personnel should make
every effort to contact the teacher or group making the visit,
to determine the value of the trip. Pertinent information
should be noted on the card.

At the end of each school year a summary of

class visits and favorable reactions should be sent to each
company visited, with appreciation noted for the availability
of the company or agency resources to the schools. If desirable, a request can be made at this time for a continua-
tion of the visiting arrangements and the form sent once
again, so that company or agency changes in personnel,
address, phone, or procedures may be noted. Where changes
in information are extensive new cards should be made.

Human Resources

        The wealth of human experience, occupations, talents
and hobbies represented by the families of the students in
any elementary school is an untapped goldmine of knowledge
of which schools in the past have made little use. Second
graders would gain a far greater appreciation of their visit
to the bakery if they were first given an opportunity to watch
a mother bake one of her prize cakes in the school's kitchen.
Fourth graders might gain greater insight into the difficulties
faced by the pioneers if they could observe an expert churn
butter, make soap, or spin wool into thread (and hopefully
be given an opportunity to try their hand at these skills).
The talent of a great singing star would be more readily
recognized if students could hear first hand from one who
knows the arduous hours of practice required to achieve such
excellence. The list is endless and the opportunities bound-
less for bringing the school and the community together
through the use of these untapped resources.

        The best place to begin locating human resources is
within the school itself. A simple questionnaire sent home
with each student will usually bring gratifying results.

SAMPLE QUESTIONNAIRE

        Dear Patron:

            Would you be willing to share your occupation,
        hobby, talents, experience or travels with the boys
        and girls of _____ School? If
        you are able to give us a little of your time, we
        feel sure that the experience would be a real learn-
        ing opportunity for students. We would be most
        grateful if you would complete the items below and
        return this questionnaire to the school.

Thank you,

_____Principal

Name_____

Address_____

Phone_____

Please note the area which you would be willing to share:

Occupation_____

Hobby   _____

Travels   _____

Other   _____

             _____

For what age level would your talk or demonstration be most suited?

_____

When might you be available to visit the school?

Day(s) _____   Time(s)_____

How far in advance do you wish to be contacted?

_____

     The organization of the human resource file should be similar to that of the community resource file. The main entry card should be under the name of the person to be contacted with an accompanying subject card. A sample card might be as follows:

       Waters, Mrs. Pauline
       222 W. Haven St.
       O'Fallon, Mo.   63366
       Phone: 272-3845

       Available: M, T   1.:00-3:00
       Age Group: 7 & up

       Subject: MEXICO: DESCRIPTION and
                 TRAVEL

The accompanying subject card would carry the heading, MEXICO: DESCRIPTION and TRAVEL. As in the case of the community resources file, one person should have the responsibility for the human resource file, noting dates and pertinent information concerning visits on the reverse side of the card. If this is not done, and teachers and students are given the responsibility for contacting those whose names are listed in the file, one person may be contacted several times for visits when one visit might take care of the needs of more than one class. In like manner, if a visit is not successful this can be noted and the card withdrawn or the factors which made the visit unsuccessful eliminated, if possible, before the next contact. If more extensive information is desired on the card, the questionnaire which is sent home can be made far more specific, listing a number of occupations, hobbies, and travels and providing space for a brief description of the presentation. This more specific listing is often desirable, for without it many people do not consider talents such as cooking or sewing valuable experiences to share. Similarly, the midwesterner who now lives in the East may not realize that his background and a description of his state or home community might prove interesting and informative to students who have never seen the midwest. If a more specific listing is called for, it should be compiled by a committee of teachers and media personnel and be related to the elementary curriculum where possible.

Bringing the Community Into the Classroom

No matter how talented or interesting a speaker or a demonstration may be, the experience will be lost on most students without prior preparation. The best time for a visit is at the end of a unit of study. Students, through independent inquiry, have by this time researched the topic, shared information, debated opinions and verified conclusions through the use of a wide variety of print and non-print sources. With a basic understanding of the topic, the new information brought by the class visitor can be integrated with what the student already knows, as illustrated in this representative project:

A fifth grade teacher noted with interest her students' discussion of the problems their parents were having with income tax forms. The class had previously studied taxation as a part of a unit in social studies class on American history. She noted that one human resource listed in the file was a tax consultant, and she asked the librarian to contact him for a visit one week later.

The teacher then obtained twenty-five short forms for declaring income tax from the local post office. The next week of math classes was spent in filling out these forms, with each student determining the income with which he wanted to work and figuring his own tax.

When the visitor arrived he was besieged with questions concerning standard deductions, tax tables and a host of other items. His comments were enthusiastically received by the young "taxpayers, " who not only appreciated his knowledge and skill, but had a hard-earned understanding of his comments concerning taxes!

Taking the Classroom to the Community

Once again, children should never be taken on a field trip "cold. " If the experience is to be valuable, considerable preparation is needed. A thorough subject of the study at hand should be undertaken. Both individual students and groups of students should be assigned responsibility for gathering information on specific aspects of the subject and for presenting it in an interesting and easily understandable manner. Careful attention should be given to terminology and specific processes to assure student understanding or intelligent questioning during the visit. A visit by the teacher before the class trip will add valuable insight and information in preparing students for the trip. Most schools require parental permission before taking students on field trips and this should be secured, usually through the use of a standard form which is sent home for parent signature. If transportation is required, it is usually the responsibility of the classroom teacher to contact the school transportation department and make the necessary arrangements.

On the trip itself, if cameras or tape recorders are allowed, they can prove most useful for securing a visual and/or audio record of the visit.

Follow-Up Activities

The class visit to the community is neither the beginning nor the end of the learning activity but an integral
part of it. On the days following the visit, time should be
devoted to recalling observations, viewing films of the visit
if pictures were taken, listening once again to the recorded
portions of the trip, and comparing the new concepts gained
with those which were held before the trip. The most successful field trip raises new questions for investigation and,
if interest has been sufficiently motivated and maintained,
students should welcome the opportunity for further investigation.

Nature Study Trips

Some areas in or near the community require no
previous contact for arranging a class visit. Parks and
wooded areas near the school or which may be a part of
the school property are cases in point. Previous preparation for these visits might be made by the science teacher
who marks a trail for students to follow with removable
markers and prepares a tape recording describing each area
of interest. Such areas might include specific types of trees
or shrubs or unusual rock formations. If wildlife was cited
on an earlier visit, students might be alerted on the tape as
to the type of wildlife to watch for. One enterprising science teacher visited the nature area at night and recorded
the sounds of night birds and insects. Students were amazed
at how quiet the same area was in the daytime.

School Camps

A number of schools, such as the Lindbergh School
District in St. Louis County, Missouri, maintain camping
facilities for students. In the spring and fall all fifth grade
students are given the opportunity to spend two weeks at the
camp, which is located some distance from the school. For
many of these suburban youngsters it is the first time they
have spent any length of time in a natural setting. Because
camping is considered to be a learning experience, the media
center also goes to camp. Books, recordings and filmstrips
on nature study are supplied in abundance so that student
curiosity can be quickly satisfied. Media personnel are also
on duty at the camp and develop an appreciation of nature

and of literature through delightful stories told around a
campfire at night.

Conference Calls

For a surprisingly small cost, conference calls to a
school can be arranged to bring students together with experts who may, because of distance, never be able to visit
the school. Many authors, actors, congressmen, scientists,
statesmen, and famous people in other occupations are willing to speak to students by phone if prior arrangement is
made. Such arrangements should include informing the
speaker of the topic or problem under discussion and inviting
his comments on it; student preparation of questions for the
speaker and provision for recording answers; and arranging
the time and place of the call. In the least expensive type
of conference call, the telephone company can arrange re-
ception via loud-speaker, so that a number of students can
hear; but only one person at a time can answer the speaker
through a single phone. This is one reason for having
questions prepared in advance and for assigning one person
to ask the questions.

Exchange of Letters and Tape Recordings

The communication boundaries of both school and
community can be broadened through the exchange of letters
and cassette recordings with students in other areas of the
United States or with students throughout the world. For a
number of years the Parker Pen Company has sponsored a
classroom-to-classroom student letter exchange program
which has been highly successful in helping students in one
part of the country or world achieve friendships and understanding of students in other parts of the world. Informal
letter exchange programs are often begun by teachers who
contact teacher friends in widely separated areas. Here
again, the personnel of the media center can play an important part in establishing such a program. A survey of
teachers throughout a school district will reveal a large
number who have contacts with teachers in other parts of
the world. A master file of these names can be established,
with a subject heading card for the state or country where
the contact is located. Pre-arrangement letters and replies
can also be kept on file to give faculty members and students
additional information in determining the area or class to

which they wish to write. When the file is established and
the contact areas have been determined, media center materials should be checked to determine the availability of
print and non-print media on the relevant geographic loca-
tions. Additional material should be purchased if collections
are lacking in the appropriate areas.

Community Surveys and Interviews

If learning is to be relevant it should be based on
current issues presented on a level of understanding appropriate to elementary students. Community involvement by
students is both desirable and needed. For this reason the
media center should subscribe to all local papers and students should be made aware of local issues important to them
and their families. One example of such a local issue centered around the proposal of a large road-building firm to
establish a quarry and asphalt plant near an elementary
school in a rather small community. The issue was hotly
debated in the local newspapers, with one paper pointing out
the disadvantages of pollution, blasting damage to homes,
danger to students at the school from increased heavy traffic,
and danger to wells in the area. The other local paper
stressed the additional taxes that the establishment of the
new industry would bring to the community. Sixth grade
students did much background reading on quarry operations
and found that they were essential if highways were to be
built. Several students volunteered to interview community
leaders and local citizens to determine their reactions to the
proposal. Other students interviewed persons who lived near
an asphalt plant in a nearby community. Citizens were
amazed at the questions asked by these knowledgeable youngsters, and when student interviews were completed and results
compiled and studied, it was concluded that the disadvantages
of the operation in this case outweighed the advantages.
Both the community interviews and the background information
found in the media center played a part in the intelligent conclusions reached by the class. It might be added that media
center personnel were required in this case to contact local
and state libraries to obtain enough information on the topic,
and these interlibrary loans provided a wealth·of material
for the student researchers.

Opportunities for Community Service

In 1954 the National Education Association gave added support to the basic goals of education formulated by the U. S. Office of Education in 1918. Among these goals were achieving self-realization by the individual and fostering citizenship and civic responsibility. There is no better way for boys and girls to achieve full citizenship in a democratic society than through community service. Many service groups exist for elementary students, including the Young Men's and Young Women's Christian Association, The Boy Scouts and Girl Scouts, The Red Cross, Junior Firemen Programs, local church groups, Campfire Girls, and local groups established to promote conservation. Most of these groups operate independently of the schools, their activities taking place in other areas and at times when school is not in session. But support for community service programs should be as much a part of the curriculum of the schools as reading or mathematics. The materials center should contain numerous materials on these service organizations and should support their programs by providing youthful members with media necessary for successful completion of projects. Materials should be available to assist scouts working on merit badges (many of which require community involvement). Books, recordings and filmstrips detailing the work and activities of the firemen should be available to the boys who join the Junior Fireman program; background reading on the Red Cross and other service organizations will help students to appreciate the work of these organizations and to feel a pride in helping to carry on that work.

The emergence of local groups interested in pollution, ecology and conservation during this decade has created a demand on the materials center for media concerned with air, water, land and sound pollution, as well as problems of overpopulation, disappearing wildlife and industrial waste. The best citizen is the informed citizen and it is a major responsibility of media personnel to see that students have the information they need--when they need it.

While it is possible to gain a vicarious understanding of community life and problems through reading, research, debate, discussion, and through the use of non-print materials, the vicarious experience is never as meaningful as direct involvement. Students can only achieve self-realization and civic responsibility through direct involvement with the community. The schools in general and media personnel

in particular must make every effort to eliminate the
structural and organizational barriers which at the present
prohibit or restrict such involvement.

Appendix A

COMMERCIAL MATERIALS AVAILABLE
FOR TEACHING WORK/STUDY SKILLS

The following materials are recommended for use in
helping students to develop efficient work/study skills. The
recommendations are based on the effectiveness of the materials in actual use with students.

Filmstrips

LITERATURE FOR CHILDREN.   Pied Piper Productions.
12 filmstrips with cassettes or records.
Each filmstrip introduces a specific type of children's liter-
ature and provides opportunity for development of literature
appreciation and locational skills.   Contents: Series One--
Story of a Book, Biography, Tall Tales, Fantasy.   Series
Two--Animals, Distant Lands, Fairy Tales, Humor. Series
Three--Enjoying Illustrations, Historical Fiction, Myths and
Adventure.

THE SCHOOL LIBRARY.   McGraw Hill Films. 6 filmstrips.
Designed for older children (grades 5-9) this set introduces
basic library and research procedures.   Titles include: The
Card Catalog, The Dictionary - Part One, The Dictionary -
Part Two, The Dewey Decimal System, The Encyclopedia,
Using Books.

USING THE ELEMENTARY SCHOOL LIBRARY.   SVE, 1968.
6 sound filmstrips, available with records or cassettes.
A series designed for grades 3-6 including: Exploring the
Library, Getting to Know Books, How to Use the Card Cata-
log, How to Use the Encyclopedia, Skills in Gathering Facts,
What's in the Dictionary.

TAPE RECORDINGS

LIBRARY AND REFERENCE SKILLS.   Creative Visuals,

151

1972.   10 tapes with accompanying student worksheets.
Care of Books (K-2)
The Story of the Lost Book (1-3)
Flip the Flea: Or a Flip Through the Card Catalog (4-9)
The Haunted Library: The Dewey Decimal System (4-9)
Facts Are Where You Find Them: Reference Books (4-9)
The Kingdom of Disorganization: Organizational Skills (4-9)
Expedition: Library Behavior (4-9)
Quiz Yourself: The Dictionary (4-9)
Quiz Yourself: The Encyclopedia (4-9)
Just Suppose: Using Nonbook Materials (4-9)

LIBRARY SKILLS.   Tapes Unlimited, 1969.   5 tapes.
Useful for primary grades.   The titles include:
  Enjoyment of Fiction
  Card Catalogue
  Dewey Decimal System
  Introduction to the Library
  Nonbook Materials

Transparencies

BASIC LIBRARY SKILLS.   Milliken Publishing Company.
  12 transparencies and 24 student worksheets in booklet
  form.
A functional approach to developing work study skills.   Skills
are introduced with full color transparencies and reinforced
through student use of the worksheets.   Worksheets require
students to use library resources.   Suitable for grades 4-8.

PRIMARY LIBRARY SKILLS.   Milliken Publishing Company.
  12 transparencies and 24 worksheets in booklet form.
Useful for introducing primary students to the library.   Develops primary library skills through the use of full color
transparencies and functional student worksheets.   Comprehensive teacher's guide.   Grades 1-4.

USING THE LIBRARY INSTRUCTIONAL MATERIALS CENTER
EFFECTIVELY.
  Creative Visuals.   64 transparencies (approximately 124
  visuals) with teacher's guide.
Basic areas covered are:
  Library Citizenship (6 transparencies) K-4
  Parts of a Book (5 transparencies) 3-5
  Finding Fiction (3 transparencies) 3-6
  Finding Nonfiction (6 transparencies) 4-8

The Card Catalog (5 transparencies) 4-8
The Dictionary (4 transparencies) 5-10
Basic Reference Tools (11 transparencies) 5-10
Using Nonbook Materials (7 transparencies) 4-8
Organizing Information (8 transparencies) 4-8
History of Books and Writing (9 transparencies) 5-10

Directory of Suppliers

CREATIVE VISUALS, P. O. Box 1911, Big Spring, Texas 79720.

MCGRAW-HILL FILMS, 330 W. 42nd St. , New York, New York 10036.

MILLIKEN PUBLISHING COMPANY, 611 Olive St. , St. Louis, Missouri 63101.

PIED PIPER PRODUCTIONS, P. O. Box 320, Verdugo City, California 91046.

SOCIETY FOR VISUAL EDUCATION, 1345 Diversey Parkway, Chicago, Illinois 60614.

TAPES UNLIMITED, 13001 Puritan Ave. , Detroit, Michigan 48227.

Appendix B

A BASIC CASSETTE TAPE COLLECTION
FOR THE ELEMENTARY SCHOOL

This list of approximately 750 cassette tapes is designed to provide the nucleus of a tape collection for the
elementary materials center. Publishers' or dealers' addresses are included for the purpose of obtaining most current catalogs and price lists.

Tapes were selected on the basis of:

(1) Curriculum need;
(2) Suitability for age and grade level indicated;
(3) Authority and authenticity;
(4) Scope;
(5) Recency of material;
(6) Technical quality.

BASIC REFERENCE SKILLS

Library and Reference Skills (k-2). Creative Visuals.
2 tapes: Library Citizenship and Care of Books.

Library and Reference Skills (3-6). Creative Visuals.
4 tapes: Haunted Library (Dewey) Flip the Flea (card catalog), Basic reference tools, Kingdom of Disorganization.

Map Study (4-6). Creative Studies.
6 tapes: introducing basic Map skills.

LANGUAGE ARTS

Grammar and Spelling

Basic Elementary English Skills (2-6). Ed. Activities.
5 tapes: Sentences, phrases, parts of speech.

154

Keys to Pronunciation (4-6).   Creative Visuals.
4 tapes: Rules for vowels, syllabication, word pronunciation.

Parts of Speech (4-6).   Creative Visuals.
6 tapes: Promotes understanding and use of nouns, pro-
nouns, adjectives, adverbs, conjunctions, prepositions.

Reading Readiness - Phonics (1-4).   Ed. Activities.
15 tapes: Initial Consonants, consonant digraphs, long and
short vowels, sound-sight skills, word recognition skills.

Learning Basic Skills through Music (k-2).   Kimbo.
4 tapes: Introducing concepts of alphabet and vocabulary.

Literature

American Folktales and Legends (4-6).   Ed. Reading Service.
6 tapes: American tall tale heroes--Paul Bunyan, Rip Van
Winkle, Pecos Bill, Johnny Appleseed, John Henry.

Experiencing Poetry (3-6).   Creative Studies.
4 tapes: Sights and sounds of poetry.

Literature for Children (k-6).   Ed. Activities.
68 tapes: Early childhood stories.   Tales of Grimm, Ander-
sen, Irving, Twain, Kipling.

Mythology of Greece and Rome (4-6).   S. V. E.
8 tapes: Legends of Greek and Roman Gods and Heroes.

Newbery Award Books (4-6).   Miller Brody Prod.
20 tapes: Accurate dramatizations of award winning childrens'
books including Johnny Tremain, Sounder, etc.

The Right Book for You (4-6).   Creative Visuals.
6 tapes: Reviews of nearly 100 books popular with students
today.   Including humor, distant lands, fantasy, realistic
fiction, history, biography.

SCIENCE, HEALTH, MATHEMATICS

Amusing Animals (k-3).   Ed. Activities.
1 tape: educational animal songs.

Animals Everywhere Series (1-6).   Creative Studies.
48 tapes: simple animals, insects, reptiles & amphibians,
fish, birds, mammals.

Discovering through Science (4-6).   Imperial Tapes.
20 tapes: animals, planets, weather, atmosphere, cells,
water, moon, plants, insects, atoms, matter, earth,
machines, stars, sound, light, sun.

Learning Basic Skills through Music - Health - Safety (k-2).
Kimbo.
1 tape: safety habits, cleanliness, posture, exercise.

Let's Find Out (1-3).   Imperial Tapes.
20 tapes: water, magnets, animals, air, land, weather,
plants, seasons, earth, sky, farm, sound, friction, desert,
moon, ocean, trees, electricity.

Products of America (3-6).   Creative Studies.
24 tapes: milk, wheat, cotton, wool, corn, fish, oil, lumber,
iron, coal, plastic, peanuts, rice, potatoes, apples, honey,
soybeans, oranges, poultry, cattle, aluminum, sugar, salt,
gold.

Programmed Mathematics (k-6).   Creative Studies.
84 tapes: sequential series in development of math skills.

Safety First Series (k-3).   Creative Studies.
9 tapes: cover safety at home, school, play.

Science Tapes (4-6).   3M Co.
12 tapes: metamorphosis, skeletal system, muscular system, buds, seedless plants, heart, states of matter, sound,
food, vision, the elements, plants with seeds.

Time to Learn - Science Tapes (3-6).   Ed. Reading Service.
24 tapes: ants, animals homes, airplanes, automobiles,
birds, bats, bees, caves, comets, computers, dogs, ele-
phants, fish, glass, glands, space stations, plastic, planets,
radar, reptiles & amphibians, steel, teeth, television,
geology.

World of Science (1-6).   Creative Studies.
24 tapes: animal babies, air, land around us, weather,
magnets, water, seasons, sound, friction, moon, trees,
electricity, ocean, desert, motion, plants, sky, cells, insects, atoms & molecules, wheel, minerals, sun, chemistry.

SOCIAL STUDIES

The United States

Exploration and Discovery (3-6).   Creative Studies.
12 tapes: Major explorers: Byrd, Cortez, Bridger, Perry,
Pike, Magellan, Marco Polo, Livingstone, Stanley, Drake,
Columbus, Coronado.

Indian Tribes (3-6).   Creative Studies.
24 tapes: each on life and customs of famous tribes.

Legacy of America (4-6).   S. V. E.
20 tapes: Covering major events in American History from
Colonial period to Modern age.

Let's Go to a Police Station (2-4).   Ed. Reading Service.
1 tape: daily activities of police.

Living With Others I and II (k-6).   Kimbo.
2 tapes: learning to be responsible citizens in home, family
and community.

My World (k-2).   S. V. E.
2 tapes: home, school, neighborhood, country life.

Our Constitution and Government (4-6).   Creative Studies.
24 tapes: Basic principles of local, state and national
government.

Teaching Manners and Behavior (k-2).   Kimbo. 1 tape.

Transportation and Communication (3-6).   Ed. Activities.
2 tapes: History of transportation and communication.

Our Fifty States (4-6).   Creative Studies.
50 tapes: Heritage of the past, today's vitality, indicators
for future growth of each state.

Westward Ho and This Land of Ours (k-2).   Kimbo.
2 tapes: to develop understanding of the U. S. and the Old
West.

What is a Congressman?   What is a Senator?   (3-6).   Ed.
Reading Service.
2 tapes: describe daily activities and duties of Congressman and Senator.

Other Lands

Africa Study Series (4-6).   Creative Studies.
18 tapes: on all countries of Africa--people and customs.

Ancient Civilizations (4-6).   Ed. Reading Service.
8 tapes: Mesopotamia, Greece, Rome, Arab Empire, Middle Ages.

Canada Series (3-6).   Creative Studies.
12 tapes: all Canadian provinces.

Christmas All Over the World (3-6).   S. V. E.
4 tapes: including Christmas customs from Ireland, Germany, Sweden, Austria, Wales, Italy, Japan, Norway and many other countries.

Viva Mexico (4-6).   Imperial' Tapes.
6 tapes: on history, culture, sports, education, etc. of Mexico.

World Travels Series (3-6).   Creative Studies.
36 tapes: interesting facts on 36 major countries of the world; Russia, England, India, etc.

Biography

American Presidents (4-6).   Imperial Tapes.
37 tapes: on lives and accomplishments of U. S. Presidents.

Black Contributors to American Culture (4-6).   S. V. E.
8 tapes: portraying lives of famous Negroes in fields of science, government, music and art.

Great Inventors Series (3-6).   Creative Studies.
24 tapes: on lives and accomplishments of famous inventors.

Time to Listen (3-6).   Ed. Reading Service.
8 tapes: Lives of Buffalo Bill, Drew, Cortez, Blackwell, Osceola, Bunche, T. Marshall, Squanto.

MUSIC

Music Masters Series (4-6).   Ed. Record Sales.
15 tapes: on lives of famous composers; Bach, Handel, Wagner, etc.

Cassette Tape Collection 159

Stories of American Patriotic Songs (3-6). Kimbo. 1 tape.

3M Music Series (4-6). 3M.
5 tapes: percussion instruments, woodwinds, strings, brass, alphabet of music.

Addresses of Companies

CREATIVE STUDIES, INC. (ESP), P. O. Box 830, 97404
Belvan Ave., San Bernardino, California. 92410

CREATIVE VISUALS, Box 1911, Big Spring, Texas 79720

EDUCATIONAL ACTIVITIES, P. O. Box 392, Freeport,
New York 11520

EDUCATIONAL READING SERVICE, 320 Rt. 17, Mahwah,
New Jersey 07430

EDUCATIONAL RECORD SALES, 157 Chambers St., New
York, N. Y. 10007

IMPERIAL TAPES, Kankakee, Illinois.

KIMBO EDUCATIONAL, P. O. Box 246, Deal, New Jersey
07723.

MILLER BRODY PRODUCTIONS, New York, N. Y. 10017.

SOCIETY FOR VISUAL EDUCATION, 1345 Diversey Parkway, Chicago, Illinois 60614.

3M COMPANY, 16th and Washington, St. Louis, Missouri.
63101

Appendix C

A BASIC FILMSTRIP COLLECTION
FOR THE ELEMENTARY SCHOOL

This list of over 400 filmstrips is designed to provide the nucleus of a filmstrip collection for the elementary
school. It is by no means an inclusive list that will serve
all the varied demands of students and teachers to the fullest
extent. However, the list supplies basic needs in most
areas of the curriculum and serves as a beginning collection
which can be expanded as the necessity for additional materials is felt and as funds become available.

In the following list, P = Primary Grades; I =
Intermediate.

ART

Fine Art in the National Gallery. 315-M. Imperial Film.
4 filmstrips. Italian Renaissance, Dutch Renaissance, the
18th and 19th Centuries, the 19th and early 20th Century.

Introducing Art Techniques. Group I, No. 327-M. Group II,
No. 328-M. Imperial Films.
12 filmstrips. Clay figures, clay pottery, creative collages,
hand puppets, finger painting, paper mosaics, cardboard &
collagraph printing, leaf and clay printing, linoleum and
woodcut printing, silk screen printing, string and glue printing, vegetable and gadget printing. (P-I)

LANGUAGE ARTS

Grammar, Spelling, Handwriting

Basic Primary Phonics. 118-SS. Group I, Group II,
Group III. SVE.
18 filmstrips covering beginning sounds, vowel sounds,
blends, rhyming words, etc. (P-I)

160

Constructing Reports. #7620. EBEC.
6 filmstrips. Research Skills, Choosing a Theme, Building
Sentences, Using and Finishing Reports, Use of Words. (I)

Goals in Spelling. #114000. McGraw-Hill.
6 filmstrips. Hearing Sounds, Consonant Sounds, Vowel
Sounds, Blends. (I)

Step-by-Step Handwriting. 121-S. SVE.
2 filmstrips. Upper and lower case letters. (P-I)

Using Good English. 130-S. SVE.
6 filmstrips. Sentence structure, plurals, contractions,
possessives, capitalization, letter writing, writing reports.
(P-I)

Your Dictionary and How to Use It. 125-S. SVE.
6 filmstrips on alphabetizing, word location, definitions,
pronunciation and syllabication. (P-I)

LITERATURE

American Folklore. Si66. Coronet.
6 filmstrips, 3 records. Paul Bunyon, Mike Fink, Pecos
Bill, Joe Magarac, John Henry, Casey Jones. (I)

Children's Classics. 122-SAR. SVE.
4 filmstrips. Three Billy Goats Gruff, Four Musicians,
Little Red Hen, The Town Mouse and Country Mouse. (P)

Children's Fairy Tales. 111-SR. SVE.
6 filmstrips. Cinderella, Snow White, Sleeping Beauty,
Little Engine that Could, Rackety Rabbit and the Runaway
Easter Eggs. (P)

Children's Stories. 107-SR. SVE.
6 filmstrips. Little Red Riding Hood, Three Little Pigs,
Gingerbread Boy, Three Bears, Rumplestiltskin, Thanks-
giving for a King. (P)

Heroes of Greek Mythology. #1930. Jam Handy.
6 filmstrips. Ulysses in the Cave of the Cyclops, Jason
and the Golden Fleece, Golden Apples of the Hesperides,
Orpheus and Eurydice, Pegasus and Bellerophon, Daedalus
and Icarus. (I)

162   Developing Methods of Inquiry

Tales by Rudyard Kipling.   Spoken Arts.
4 filmstrips.   How the Whale Got His Throat, How the
Camel Got His Hump, How the Rhinoceros Got His Skin,
The Elephant's Child.   (I)

MATHEMATICS

Fundamentals of Modern Math.   #3150.   Jam Handy.
10 filmstrips.   Sets, whole numbers, integers, rational
numbers, relations, functions, finite mathematical systems,
numeration systems, shapes, areas.   (I)

Introduction to Fractions.   #1030.   Jam Handy.
5 filmstrips.   Introducing fractional concepts.   (I)

Mathematics for Primary Grades.   #1020.   Jam Handy.
8 filmstrips.   Story of Numbers, Comparing Sizes, Matching
Numbers, Meaning of Numbers 1-10, What One Half Means,
Measuring How Long, Measuring How Much.   (P)

MUSIC

Music Stories.   #1750.   Jam Handy.
6 filmstrips w/records.   Peter and the Wolf, Hansel and
Gretel, The Nutcracker, Peer Gynt, The Firebird, The
Sorcerer's Apprentice.   (P-I)

Our Heritage of American Folk Music.   681-SAR, 681-SBR.
SVE.
12 filmstrips w/records.   Music of sea, cowboys, mountains, plains, railroad, Civil War, American Revolution,
Old South, pioneer mid-America, Western Frontier, Missis-
sippi Valley, old Southwest.   (P-I)

Stories of Music Classics.   #1770.   Jam Handy.
6 filmstrips w/records.   Sleeping Beauty, William Tell, A
Midsummer Night's Dream, Swan Lake, The Bartered Bride,
Scheherazade.   (I)

PHYSICAL EDUCATION

Physical Fitness.   571-S.   SVE.
4 filmstrips.   Fitness and exercises, team games, self-
testing, rhythmic activities.   (P-I)

Soccer. 604-SR. Tumbling. 586-SR. SVE.
6 filmstrips, 4 records. (I)

Track and Field. 574-SR. SVE.
3 filmstrips, 2 records. (I)

SCIENCE AND HEALTH

General Science

Preparing Your Science Project. EBEC. (I)

Exhibiting Your Science Project. EBEC. (I)

Astronomy

Astronomy in the Space Age. #207. Eyegate.
8 filmstrips on the sun, moon, earth, solar system, stars,
space travelers, tools of astronomers. (I)

The Earth and Its Neighbors in Space. #8410. EBEC.
6 filmstrips covering the earth, moon, solar system, stars,
astronomy through the ages. (I)

Finding Out About Day and Night. 424-12. SVE. (P)

Finding Out About the Sky. 424-6. SVE. (P)

Finding Out About the Solar System. 424-17. SVE. (P)

Biology

Ecology of a Seashore. #434-1. Imperial Films. (I)

The Vocabulary of Biology. Group I: The Invertebrates.
#646M. Imperial Films.
6 filmstrips. Protozoans, Sponges, Flatworms, Mollusks,
Arthropods, Insects. (I)

Botony

Learning About Plants. #9430. EBEC.
6 filmstrips. Plant Needs, Parts of a Plant, Seeds, Plants
We Use. (P)

Plant Structure and Growth.   #3020.   Jam Handy.
8 filmstrips.   Characteristics of Plants, Plant Cells, Photo-
synthesis, Roots, Stems and Leaves, From Flower to Seed,
Germination, Nongreen Plants, Adaptations.   (I)

Chemistry

Elementary Chemistry.   #427SF.   SVE.
3 filmstrips.   What Things Are Made Of, Chemical Changes,
Atoms and Molecules.   (I)

Understanding Chemical Change.   #58-2763.   McGraw-Hill. (I)

Geology

First Experiments About Weather.   #1060.   Jam Handy.
6 filmstrips.   What is an Experiment, How Does Water Get
into the Air, What Makes Things Dry Faster, Where Do
Clouds Come From, What is Wind, Why is Night Cooler
than Day.   (P)

Life Long Ago.   431-SA.   SVE.
6 filmstrips.   Development of Reptiles, Mammals, Fossils,
etc.   (I)

Physiographic Changes.   431-SC.   SVE.
6 filmstrips.   Changing Face of the Earth, Rivers of Water
and Ice, Underground Water, Volcanoes and Earthquakes,
Mountains.   (I)

Rocks and Minerals.   435-11.   SVE.   (P)

Rocks and Minerals.   431-SB.   SVE.
4 filmstrips.   Earth's Crust, Common Minerals, Earth, a
Great Storehouse, Earth's Diary.

Seasons, Weather and Climate.   #1240.   Jam Handy.
5 filmstrips.   Our Earth in Motion, The Sun and Our Seasons, What is Weather, What Makes Weather, Climate. (I)

Understanding Oceanography.   503-SR.   SVE.
6 filmstrips.   Study of Oceans, Ocean Basins, Characteristics of Sea Water, Currents and Tides, Life in the Open
Seas, Life on the Sea Floor and Shore. (I)

Health and Safety

Health Stories. #7760. EBEC.
6 filmstrips. Health Habits, Checking Your Health, Keeping
Neat and Clean, Avoiding Infection, Proper Food, Health
Helpers. (P)

Learning About Health. #6426. EBEC.
9 filmstrips. Health Questions, Teeth, Ears, Eyes, Skin,
Food, Exercise, Neatness, Germs. (P)

Systems of the Human Body. Ed. Act. Inc.
6 filmstrips. Skeletal, Muscular, Digestive, Nervous,
Respiratory, Circulatory. (I)

Safety Tales. #8790. EBEC.
6 filmstrips. Accidents, Bicycle Safety, Fire Prevention,
Accident Prevention. (P)

Living Things

Animal Differences. #422-3. Imperial Films. (I)

Birds You Should Know. #092475. McGraw Hill.
4 filmstrips. Owls, the Kingfisher, Birds of the City,
Hawks. (P-I)

Different Kinds of Animals. #9410. EBEC.
6 filmstrips. Mammals, Birds, Amphibians, Reptiles, Insects, Water Animals. (P)

Dolphins and Sea Lions. #407-5. Imperial Films. (I)

Learning About Living Things. #10970. EBEC.
6 filmstrips. Relationships Among Living Things, Food
Needs, How Life Continues. (P)

Our Pets. #400185. McGraw Hill.
6 filmstrips. The Parakeet, the Pony, the Kitten, the
Rabbit, the Puppy, the Turtle. (P)

Underwater Animals. #407-4. Imperial Films. (I)

Physics

Heat, Light and Sound. #1200. Jam Handy.
7 filmstrips. Nature of Heat, Expansion, How Heat Travels,

Light and Color, Nature of Sound, How Sound Travels. (I)

Simple Machines Help Us Work.   #1080.   Jam Handy.
6 filmstrips.   Levers, Wheels, Pulleys, Ramps, Wedges,
Screws.   (P)

Understanding Electricity.   #1210.   Jam Handy.
7 filmstrips.   Static Electricity, Current Electricity, How
Electricity is Produced, Electromagnets, Safety.   (I)

Work, Friction and Machines.   #1190.   Jam Handy.
6 filmstrips.   Work and Friction, Inclined Planes, Levers,
Pulleys, Wheels, Screws.   (I)

SOCIAL STUDIES

American History

American Indians.   S151, S194, S214, S110, S150. Coronet.
30 filmstrips, 14 records.   Southwest Indian Families,
American Indians of North Pacific Coast, American Indian
Legends, American Indians of the Northeast, American Indians of the Southwest.   (I)

Living in Colonial America.   615-M.   Imperial Films.
6 filmstrips.   Living in Early Plymouth, Massachusetts;
Jamestown, Virginia; 18th Century New England; 18th Century
Virginia; Colonial Williamsburg; Homes of Washington and
Jefferson.   (I)

People and Events in American History.   Imperial Films.
12 filmstrips.   Our Independence & the Constitution, Lewis
& Clark, The California Gold Rush, Ben Franklin, Daniel
Boone, Robert Fulton, The First Trans-Continental Railroad,
Pere Marquette, Pony Express, The Wright Brothers, The
Panama Canal.   (I)

Pioneers of the Early American Frontier.   234-S.   SVE.
4 filmstrips.   The Trip Westward, The New Home, Life in
the Wilderness, New Neighbors and A New Town.   (P-I)

Conservation

Learning About Conservation.   #S109.   Coronet.
6 filmstrips, 3 records.   Problems We Face, Our Soil, Our
Water & Air, Our Forests, Our Grassland, Our Minerals and
Energy Resources.   (I)

Pollution. #S198. Coronet.
6 filmstrips, 3 records. Problems of air, water, land
pollution. (I)

Community Life

The City Community. #7800. EBEC.
6 filmstrips. Here is the City, Business, Living in the
City, Problems, Work, Keeping the City Alive. (P)

The Country Community. #7740. EBEC.
6 filmstrips. A Rural Village, School in the Country, The
New Fire Engine, The American Farmer, Living on a Farm,
A Country Fair. (P)

Good Manners. #8300. EBEC.
6 filmstrips. Manners at home, school, parties, play,
visiting, public. (P)

The Home Community. #7700. EBEC.
6 filmstrips. Our Family to the Rescue, Family Fun,
Keeping Busy, Helping Mother, Brothers and Sisters, Growing Up. (P)

The School Community. #7720. EBEC.
6 filmstrips. The New Pupil, Our School, School Helpers,
Our Job in School, Part of the Team, School Courtesy. (P)

The Town Community. #7780. EBEC.
6 filmstrips. This is Our Town, How Our Town Began,
How Our Town Grew, Living in Our Town, Working in Our
Town, The Future of Our Town. (P)

Government

Our National Government, How it Developed. 366-SA. SVE.
4 filmstrips. Declaration of Independence, Articles of Con-
federation, Adoption of the Constitution, Growth of the Constitution. (I)

Exploration and Discovery

Great Explorers Series. #401349, #401356, McGraw Hill.
12 filmstrips. Marco Polo, Marquette, Magellan, Cortez,
Cabot, Lewis & Clark, Columbus, Drake, Champlain, De
Soto, Coronado, Hudson. (I)

Other Lands

Ancient Civilizations. 601-1, 601-2. Imperial Films.
2 filmstrips. Exploring Ancient Athens and Exploring
Ancient Rome. (I)

Canada: Regions and Resources. 270-SF. SVE.
4 filmstrips. British Columbia and the Yukon, Prairie
Provinces, Ontario, St. Lawrence Seaway, Quebec. (I)

Cities of the World. EBEC.
8 filmstrips. Singapore, Rome: the City, Paris, London,
Glimpses of Holland, The Rhine River, Villages in Greece,
Bombay, Gateway to India. (I)

Countries of the World. SVE.
5 filmstrips. British Isles, Modern France, Modern Nether-
lands, Modern Greece, Modern Southwestern Asia. (I)

Living in Mexico Today. 273-SR. SVE.
4 filmstrips. Northern Mexico, The Historical Triangle,
Taxco, Southern Mexico. (I)

Living in South America Today. 272-SR. SVE.
6 filmstrips. Northern South America, Andean Highlands,
Amazon Basin, Brazilian Highlands, Rio de la Plata, Chile.
(I)

Seeing Central America. S128.
6 filmstrips, 3 records. Nations, Land, Agriculture, Man-
ufacturing, People, Panama Canal. (I)

Transportation

Transportation Today. #S111. Coronet.
6 filmstrips, 3 records. Water, rail, highway and air
systems. (I)

Traveling In and Out of Our City. #S149. Coronet.
4 filmstrips, 2 records. Airport, Bus Station, Railroads,
Harbor. (P)

United States: Description and Travel

Cities of Our Country. #31. Eye Gate House.
9 filmstrips. Birmingham, Los Angeles, Boston, Chicago,
How Cities Grow, Detroit, Seattle, New York, Houston. (I)

Thompson.   The Horse that Liked Sandwiches

Daugherty.   The Picnic

Arnov.   Wonders of the Deep Sea

Telfer.   About Salt, Boom-Miracle Salt, Golden-Salt

Telfer.   Watch Honeybees with Me

Watson.   Katies Chickens

Weber.   Up Above and Down Below

Kay.   Fishes

Manneheim.   Touch Me, Touch Me Not

LEARNING ABOUT MAPS AND GLOBES

Grade 4

Learning aids in the library:

Books

Hackler.   How Maps and Globes Help Us

Rinkoff.   A Map is a Picture

Epstein.   First Book of Maps and Globes

Rand-McNally.   Book of Nations

World Book Atlas

Golden Book Atlas

Hammond Nature Atlas

Answer Book of Geography

Geography of the World

The call number for books about maps is_____.

Using any of the above listed resources answer the following questions:

Define:

Latitude:
Longitude:
Equator:
Map Compass:
Mercator Map:

What are the two major uses of color on a map?

1.
2.

How many different types of maps can you name? Examples: political map, population map, etc. List the names below:

1.	7.
2.	8.
3.	9.
4.	10.
5.	11.
6.	12.

Draw and label twelve commonly used map symbols.

DISCOVERY AND EXPLORATION

Grade 5

Reading about famous men and women who crossed unknown oceans and explored strange lands can be more exciting than almost any reading you will do.

As you listen to records, view filmstrips, or read about the lives of these famous explorers decide what qualities you believe one must have to enter the world of the unknown.

There are two places to look in your school library to

find materials about famous people.   Here they are:

1. The Call Number 910 will lead you to books on dis-
    covery and exploration.

2. The biography section will contain books about the
    lives of explorers. Remember that biographies are
    shelved alphabetically by the name of the person
    written about.

TITLE	AUTHOR	TYPE OF MATERIAL
Explorers of the World	Clark, William	book
Encyclopedia of Explo- rations	Riverain, Jean	book
Roald Amundsen	Kugelmass, J. Alvin	book
Balboa	Mirsky, Jeanette	book
Cartier Sails the St. Lawrence	Averill, Esther	book
Champlain, Father of New France	Edwards, Cecile	book
Columbus, Finder of the New World	Syme, Ronald	book
Captain Cook and the South Pacific	Horizon Magazine	book
Francisco Coronado	Faith Knoop	book
Hernando Cortes	Graff, Stewart	book
Francis Drake	Syme, Ronald	book
Vasco da Gama	Syme, Ronald	book
LaSalle, River Explorer	Graham, Alberta	book
The Vikings	Janeway, Elizabeth	book
Magellan, First Around the World	Syme, Ronald	book

TITLE	AUTHOR	TYPE OF MATERIAL
Juan Ponce de Leon	Baker, Nina	book
Quesada of Columbia	Syme, Ronald	book
Amerigo Vespucci	Baker, Nina	book
Richard Byrd	Creative Studies	tape
Hernando Cortes	Creative Studies	tape
Robert E. Perry	Creative Studies	tape
Magellan, World Explorer	Creative Studies	tape
Sir Francis Drake	Creative Studies	tape
Christopher Columbus	Creative Studies	tape
Great Explorers Series	McGraw Hill	filmstrips

A CHANCE TO READ!

Grade 5

AMERICAN HISTORY

Historical Fiction

Your study of American history will be a very interesting one if you will visit your school library to discover
all of the exciting books on this subject that can be found
there. Some of the most popular books in this field are
those of historical fiction. In a book of historical fiction
most of the facts concerning the time period written about
are true; however, the central characters in the book may
be fictional as well as the conversations and some of the in-
cidents that take place. It is your job as the reader to be
able to distinguish between fact and fiction. The material
that you are studying in your social studies text will help you
to be able to do this. Your text provides a background for
the reading you are doing now and will do in the future. For

example, can you tell if these statements are fact or fiction?

1. George Washington drove down the streets of Mt. Vernon in his Jaguar.
2. Robert E. Lee led his troops to victory in the Battle of the Bulge.
3. Abraham Lincoln strove for a united country during the Civil War.

You will find exciting reading in the following books which are in your central library:

AUTHOR	TITLE	CALL NUMBER
Adams	Pony Express	_____
Adams	Santa Fe Trail	_____
Adams	Wagons to the Wilderness	_____
Beals	Davy Crockett, Kit Carson, Daniel Boone	_____
Cavanah	Our Country's Story	_____
Commager	First Book of American History	_____
Coy	The Americans	_____
Dupuy	First Book of Civil War Land Battles	_____
Foster, Meadow- craft, Judson	Abraham Lincoln	_____
Gipson	Old Yeller	_____
Lampman	Wheels West - Story of Tabitha Brown	_____
McNeer	War Chief of the Seminoles	_____
Miers	When Grant Met Lee at Appomattox	_____
Proudfit	River Boy	_____

AUTHOR	TITLE	CALL NUMBER
Rose	Clara Barton	_____

Only a few of the many good books available have been
listed.   For others consult the card catalog.   Topics to look
under in the catalog are:

United States--History
Westward Movement
Civil War
War With Mexico
Expansion U. S.
Names of Famous People
Names of Famous Places

The call numbers for nonfiction in the American history section are:

973	United States
973. 1	America--Discovery and Exploration
973. 2	Colonial Period
973. 3	Revolution and Confederation
973. 4	Constitutional Period (including Lewis & Clark, Louisiana Purchase)
973. 5	Early 19th Century--(including War of 1812)
973. 6	Middle 19th Century--(including War with Mexico)
973. 7	Civil War
973. 8	Later 19th Century
973. 9	20th Century
978	Westward Expansion
B, 92, or 920	Biography

CONSERVING OUR NATURAL RESOURCES

Grades 4-6

Unit Theme: Man is polluting his environment and
destroying his natural surroundings at an unprecedented rate.
If man is to survive he must become aware of the importance
of conserving his natural resources.

   Activity: Students will prepare a conservation notebook including:

A.   Field trip observations concerning ways to improve
     our environment.

B.   Pictures, clippings and articles on good conservation
     practices.

C.   Articles which describe the dangers to our environ-
     ment and practices which will help to eliminate the
     dangers.

Bibliography for Student Use

General

Billington, Elizabeth J.   Understanding Ecology.   Warne, 1968.

Parker, Bertha Morris.   The Golden Treasury of Natural
     History.   Golden, 1952.

Soil

Adler, Irving and Ruth.   The Earth's Crust.   Day, 1963.

Bieser, Arthur.   The Earth.   Time-Life, 1968.

Miller, M. E.   Soil Management.   Boy Scouts of America,
     1943.

National Wildlife Federation.   Nature's Bank - The Soil.   1953.

Simon, Seymour.   A Handful of Soil.   Hawthorn, 1970.

Rocks and Minerals

Adler, Irving and Ruth.   Coal.   Day, 1965.

Beiser, Arthur.   The Earth.   Time-Life, 1968.

Crosby, Phoebe.   Rock Collecting.   Garrard, 1962.

Golden Press.   Rocks and Minerals.   1957.

Hyler, Nelson.   Rocks and Minerals.   Grosset & Dunlap. 1960.

Shepherd, Walter.   Wealth from the Ground.   Day, 1962.

Swensen, Valerie.   Stones and Minerals.   Maxton, 1955.

White, Anne Terry.   All About Rocks and Minerals.   Random, 1955.

White, Anne Terry.   Rocks All Around Us.   Random, 1959.

Zim, Herbert S.   Minerals.   Harcourt Brace, 1943.

Air and Water

Adler, Irving and Ruth.   Irrigation, Changing Deserts into Gardens.   Day, 1964.

Buehr, Walter.   Water, Our Vital Need.   Norton, 1967.

Chester, Michael.   Let's Go Stop Air Pollution.   Putnam, 1968.

Davies, Delwyn.   Fresh Water.   Doubleday, 1969.

Feravolo, Rocco.   Water Experiments.   Garrard, 1965.

Golden Press.   Pond Life.   1957.

Lewis, Alfred.   Clean the Air.   McGraw-Hill, 1965.

Lindemann, Edward.   Water Animals for Your Microscope. Crowell, 1967.

Peterson, Ottis.   Junior Science Book of Water.   Garrard, 1966.

Forest

Blough, Glenn O.   Lookout for the Forest.   McGraw-Hill, 1955.

Brooks, Anita.   The Picture Book of Timber.   Day, 1967.

Caulfield, Peggy.   Leaves.   Coward-McCann, 1962.

Golden Press.   Trees, A Guide to Familiar American Trees. 1952.

Unit Bibliographies   181

Hambleton, Jack.   Fire in the Valley.   Longmans, Green &
    Co. , 1960.

Harrison, William.   Forest Fire Fighters and What They Do.
    Watts, 1962.

Hyde, Wayne.   What Does a Forest Ranger Do?   Dodd-
    Mead, 1964.

Kraft, John.   Exploring the Forest.   McGraw-Hill, 1962.

MacConomy, Alma.   Odd Jobs in Lumbering.   Putnam, 1967.

Moore, Alma.   The Friendly Forests.   Viking, 1954.

Perry, John.   Foresters and What They Do.   Watts, 1963.

Wildlife

Adrain, Mary.   The North American Wolf.   Hastings House,
    1965.

Bailey, John.   Our Wild Animals.   Nelson, 1965.

Colby, C. B.   Fish and Wildlife.   Coward-McCann, 1955.

Colby, C. B.   Wild Dogs.   Sloan and Pearce, 1965.

Hess, Lilo.   The Misunderstood Skunk.   Scribners, 1969.

Perry, Bill.   Our Threatened Wildlife.   Coward-McCann,
    1969.

Periodicals

National Geographic School Bulletin.   Published weekly dur-
    ing the school year by the National Geographic Society,
    17th and M Streets N. W. , Washington, D. C.   20036.

National Wildlife.   Published monthly by the National Wild-
    life Federation, 1412 16th St. N. W. , Washington, D. C.
    65101.

Ranger Rick.   Published monthly by the National Wildlife
    Federation, 1412 16th St. N. W. , Washington, D. C.   65101.

Filmstrips

General

What is Conservation.   Encyclopedia Britannica, 1961.

Soil

Improving Our Grasslands.   Encyclopedia Britannica, 1961.

Saving Our Soil.   Encyclopedia Britannica, 1961.

How Man Has Used the Soil.   Encyclopedia Britannica, 1950.

How Man Conserves the Soil.   Encyclopedia Britannica, 1950.

How Soil is Formed.   Encyclopedia Britannica, 1950.

Rocks and Minerals

Rocks and How They Change.   Filmstrip House, 1960.

Rocks and Minerals.   Childrens Press, 1969.

Using Our Minerals Wisely.   Encyclopedia Britannica, 1950.

Water

Enough Water for Everyone.   Encyclopedia Britannica, 1961.

Water and the Soil.   Encyclopedia Britannica, n. d.

Forest

Using Our Forest Wisely.   Encyclopedia Britannica, 1961.

Wildlife

Giving Our Wildlife a Chance.   Encyclopedia Britannica, 1961.

GREEK AND ROMAN MYTHOLOGY UNIT

Grade 6

Unit Objectives

After completing a four-week study of Greek and Roman Mythology, the child (student) should be able to:

1. Correctly match gods and goddesses and their characteristics and roles in mythology on an objective test.

2. Recognize and correctly use particular words and phrases contributed to the English language from Greek and Roman mythology.

3. Recognize themes in myths and relate them to a modern day setting and with the entire class write and produce a present day mythological play.

Activities

1. Illustrate the creation (according to myth) on a mural.

2. Using transparencies and a layering effect on an overhead projector, illustrate chaos being added to the earth. (Etc.)

3. For a child interested in stars, have him read further on astronomy and create a constellation by punching holes in paper and putting the paper on the overhead projector.

4. Look for references to myths in advertising; for example, Standard Gasoline (the winged horse); Florists (FTD) (Mercury).

5. Make a mythology dictionary including Greek and Roman words (or names), what they mean, and what words they could or do allude to in the English language.

Bibliography

Arbuthnot, May Hill, The Arbuthnot Anthology of Children's Literature, Scott, Foresman and Company, 1953. (pp. 212-237).

Asimov, Isaac, Words From Myths, Houghton Mifflin, 1961.

D'Aulaire, Ingri and Edgar, Book of Greek Myths, Doubleday, 1962.

Baldwin, James, Favorite Tales of Long Ago, Dutton, 1955.

Benson, Sally, Stories of Gods and Heroes, Dial Press, 1940.

Bulfinch, Thomas, A Book of Myths, Macmillan, 1942.

Church, Alfred, The Odyssey for Boys and Girls, Macmillan, 1930.

Colum, Padraic, The Golden Fleece and the Heroes Who Lived Before Achilles, Macmillan, 1949.

Farmer, Penelope and Conner, Chris, Daedalus and Icarus, Harcourt Brace Jovanovich, Inc., 1971.

Graves, Robert, Greek Gods and Heroes, Doubleday, 1960.

Green, Roger, Tales the Muses Told, Walck, 1965.

Hamilton, Edith, Mythology, Little, Brown, 1944.

Hawthorne, Nathaniel, Tanglewood Tales, Dutton, 1950.

_____. A Wonder Book, Dutton, 1949.

Kingsley, Charles, The Heroes; Greek Fairy Tales, Macmillan, 1954.

Mabie, Hamilton, Myths Every Child Should Know, Grosset & Dunlap, 1905.

Schreiber, Morris, Famous Myths and Legends of the World, Grosset, 1960.

Sissons, Nicola Ann, Myths and Legends of Many Lands, Hart, 1962.

White, Anne Terry, The Golden Treasury of Myths and Legends, Golden, 1962.

For Teacher Reference

Loverdo, Costa de, Gods with Bronze Swords, Doubleday, 1970.

Murray, Elizabeth, "Mythology is for Now, " Instructor, May, 1972.

Rose, H. J., Gods and Heroes of the Greeks, Meridan, 1969.

PLAY THE GAME

Grades 4-6

Directions:

Choose one of the sports or games listed below which interests you. Draw a circle around it. Use the encyclopedia to find the answers to the questions below which will tell about the sport or game you have chosen.

Archery	Gymnastics	Softball
Badminton	Handball	Surfing
Baseball	Ice Hockey	Swimming
Basketball	Judo	Table Tennis
Bowling	Lacrosse	Tennis
Boxing	Rowing	Volleyball
Fencing	Shooting	Water Skiing
Field Hockey	Skiing	Weightlifting
Football	Sky Diving	Wrestling
Golf	Soccer	Yachting

1. How many players does it take to play this?_____

2. Do you need equipment for this sport?_____ What equipment?_____

3. Where did this sport originate?_____

4. How old is this sport?_____

    5.   Is this a seasonal sport?_____

    6.   Who may play this sport?_____

    7.   Who do you consider the most famous athlete in
         this sport?_____

    8.   Is this sport mainly for girls or boys?_____

         Now find your sport in some other book in the library.
Use the card catalog or look for books on the sport shelf.
Books about sports have the numbers 790-799.

Write the title of the book here: _____

Who wrote this book?_____

When was the book written?_____

                        CHOOSE A SPORTS HERO

                            Grades 4-6

Directions:

         Choose one of the sports heroes listed below.   Draw
a circle around the name that interests you.   Use the encyclopedia or the biographical dictionary to find information
about this person.   Answer the questions below.

Bob Garrett   Willie Mays   Gretchen Fraser
Ray Ewry   Aileen Soule   Bob Feller
Felix Carvajal   Jesse Owens   Mark Spitz
Joe Louis   Floretta McCutcheon Branch Rickey
Jim Thorpe   Wilt Chamberlain   Mildred Zaharias
Sugar Ray Robinson   Carol Jenkins   Knute Rockne
Margaret Varner   James M. Brown   Joe DiMaggio
Jackie Robinson   Stan Musial   Ted Williams
Glenna Vare   Shirley Garms   Joe Namath
Leroy Paige   Althea Gibson   Ty Cobb
Wilma Rudolph   Helen Roark   Theresa Blanchard

    1.   When was this person born?_____

2. Where was this person born?_____

3. Is this person living today?_____

4. In what sport did this person achieve fame?_____

5. Exactly what did this person do to achieve fame?__
   _____
   _____

    Can you read about this person in any other book in your library? Check the biography shelf for books on sports heroes.

Name of the book_____

Author_____

HISTORICAL FICTION

"Pilgrims to Pioneers"

Grades 5-6

    Purpose: 1) to portray children and adults, both real and fictional, in historical settings extending in time from the middle 1600's up to and including the civil war period; 2) to reveal the fact that even though places and events may change, basic human characteristics tend to remain constant.

    Things to consider:

1. What other particular period of time would you liked to have lived? Why ?
2. Make a comparison of your life today to that of another time.
3. Dramatize a particular incident from one of your favorite books.
4. Exchange places with one of your favorite characters. How would you react to the problems he or she faced?
5. Construct a model of an Indian village, frontier fort, pioneer cabin or any other structure representing a certain time period.

188 Developing Methods of Inquiry

6. In historical fiction, the author may invent stories, characters and events but must not change basic historical facts. After you have read a book, try to decide which parts of the story are true and those that are not.
7. Take note of the particular time period the author is writing about as you read each book.

Sam and the Colonels by Bianca Bradbury. A 13-year-old boy plays a major role in the conspiracy to save Colonels Whalley and Goffe from Charles II. (5-7)

Towappu Puritan Renegade by Peter Stephens. Timothy Morris tries to prevent an Indian war and finds himself prisoner of the colonist of Plymouth Colony. (6-9)

The Pilgrim Goose by Keith Robertson. A history of the Pilgrim geese, covering over 300 years, gives a glimpse of what happened to them at different times in our country's history. (4-6)

The Witch of Blackbird Pond by Elizabeth Speare. Fun-loving Kit Tyler's actions lead the Puritans to believe she is a witch. She is brought to trial but saved by a small Puritan child. (6-9) Newbery Award, 1958.

Tituba of Salem Village by Anne Petry. A true story of a Negro slave accused of practicing witchcraft which comes to a climax with the famous Salem Witchcraft Trials of 1692. (6-9)

Tomahawk Border by William Steele. The story of a 16-year-old boy's fight to regain the respect of his comrades in the ranks of the Virginia rangers. (5-7)

The Cabin Faced West by Jean Fritz. A true story about the author's great-great grandmother. (4-6)

Shippack School by Marguerite de Angeli. Mischievous Eli Shrawder learns a lesson from schoolmaster Christopher Dock. (4-6)

Calico Captive by Elizabeth Speare. A story of a courageous family captured by Indians and sold into slavery in Canada just before the French and Indian War. (6-9)

The Matchlock Gun by Walter Edmonds.   Newbery Award,
1942.   French and Indian warfare against the British in New
York State gives 10-year-old Edward Van Alstyne the chance
to fire a huge Spanish gun.   (4-6)

The Light in the Forest by Conrad Richter.   True Son, a
white boy reared as an Indian, is forced to return to his
real parents which results in many conflicts.   (6-9)

Johnny Tremain by Esther Forbes.   Newbery Award, 1944.
A young silversmith's apprentice overcomes a physical handi-
cap to play an important part in the American Revolution as
a rider for the Committee of Public Safety.   (6-9)

The Rebel Courier and the Redcoats by Merle Constiner.
When the original messenger is arrested by a British "spy
catcher, " 16-year-old Clay Henderson finds himself suddenly
entrusted with a message of utmost importance from Gen.
Washington to General Gates.   (4-6)

Daughter of Liberty by Edna Boutwell.   Amy and her doll,
Polly Sumner, carry out a dangerous mission and earn the
praise of Paul Revere as true daughters of liberty.   (4-6)

The Year of the Bloody Sevens by William Steele.   When his
traveling companions are killed, 11-year-old Kel Bond strikes
out alone to join his father in Kentucky.   (4-6)

Bread-And-Butter Indian by Anne Colver.   Barbara Baum
becomes friends with an Indian who risks his life to return
her to her parents when she is captured by Indians.   (4-6)

The Lone Hunt by William Steele.   Yance Caywood's pride
in killing a buffalo is overshadowed by the loss of his well-
loved hound dog, Blue.   (4-6)

Caroline and Her Kettle Named Maud by Miriam Mason.
Caroline's disappointment in her grandfather's gift of a cop-
per kettle turns into pride when she uses it to capture a
wolf.   (3-4)

Carolina's Courage by Elizabeth Yates.   A New Hampshire
girl moves west and sacrifices her beloved doll to insure a
safe journey through Indian territory.   (4-6)

Oregon at Last! by A. Rutgers Van der Loeff.   When both
parents die along the trail, the Sager children make the in-

credible journey to Oregon by themselves. (6-9)

Thee, Hannah by Marguerite de Angeli.   Hannah's religion
takes on a new meaning for her when she helps a runaway
slave who trusts her because of her Quaker Bonnet.   (4-6)

The Undergrounders by Bianca Bradbury.   A family's experiences as they run a station on the underground railroad.
(5-7)

By Secret Railway by Enid Meadowcroft.   When Jim's freedom papers are destroyed, he is sold back into slavery but
manages to escape to freedom with help of David Morgan and
his family.   (4-6)

Riding The Pony Express by Clyde Bulla.   Dick Park keeps
the mail moving when his father, a pony express rider, is
wounded.   (3-4)

Caddie Woodlawn by Carol Ryrie Brink.   Newbery Award,
1936.   The adventures of a mischievous, daring young pioneer girl who lived in Wisconsin during Civil War days.
(5-6)

Orphans of the Wind by Erik Haugaard.   When an English
blockaide runner explodes and sinks, 12-year-old Jim and
three other sailors make it to shore and wish to join the
Union army during the Civil War.   (6-9)

The Perilous Road by William Steele.   The dangerous adventures of one boy before he learns the senseless waste of
war and the true meaning of courage and tolerance.   (5-6)

Across Five Aprils by Irene Hunt.   A moving story of a
family torn apart by the Civil War and of Jethro, 9 years
old, who runs the farm almost alone.   (6-9)

INDEX

192

194